THE LADY OF BEAUTY

AGNES SOREL

FIRST ROYAL FAVOURITE
OF FRANCE

BY JEHANNE D'ORLIAC

THE MOON MISTRESS: DIANE DE POITIERS

AGNESSOREL

AGNES SOREL: THE LADY OF BEAUTY

From the Portrait at Château de Mouchy

THE LADY OF BEAUTY
AGNES SOREL
FIRST ROYAL FAVOURITE OF FRANCE

BY JEHANNE D'ORLIAC

TRANSLATED BY
M. C. DARNTON

WITH 17 ILLUSTRATIONS

PHILADELPHIA & LONDON
J. B. LIPPINCOTT COMPANY
MCMXXXI

CONTENTS

ILLUSTRATIONS

CHAPTER I
The Damsel of Fromenteau

CHAPTER I

The Damsel of Fromenteau

EVERY one is agreed that Love alone lends enchantment to life; yet every one, when he encounters Love, also seems bent on decrying it, execrating it, sullying it. Is this strange attitude born of spite or a grudge—the spite of those whom it has betrayed, the grudge of those whom it has wounded? Few are loved in this world. Few know how to love. Yet many are loved who do not themselves know how to love; others would know how who never have the opportunity. Is it all a matter of luck or accident? Let us, then, hail those who are successful in love. They who attain that happy union in which heart and senses alike are satisfied are the darlings of the gods. Even more fortunate are those who, in the continuance of this rare harmony, can spend their lives in lasting felicity, the marvel and the envy of all. Let us not long for fortune, but for happiness. Let us not long for glory, but for love. Or glory for love.

The love of Charles VII for Agnes Sorel was one which should not be decried but lauded, set up not as a mark for scorn but as an example. We must despise those, to be sure, who confound love with adventure; those who make a free or lucrative trade of their bodies and their souls, to gain material or social advantages for themselves; courtesans of both sexes, given over to venal rather than to amorous passions; comedians and comediennes of a sentiment which they debase. We must pity those others who never find respite from the devouring fire of passion, who seek without ever finding the delights which flee them, torture and ravage them. Their cases belong to the province of pathology, not psychology. Their hysteria must not be confounded with true love, the lofty desire for a being whose possession alone can fulfil us.

The whole subject is in confusion still. The same word is applied to things that are absolutely contrary. Love is a whole. The soul and the body, the mind and the senses must all combine to make it perfect. If by a happy chance the social position of the lovers affords them the resources of luxury, if life spreads before them romantic circumstances favorable to the flowering of their love and its sublimation, then is born that masterpiece of love before which we must bow in admiration, as we do before all exceptional achievement.

There are heroes of love, as there are heroes of glory. They are marked out beforehand by special characteristics. In their presence we feel that strange agitation, at once delightful and disturbing, which makes us flee them or pursue them according to whether our hearts are bold or prudent.

Agnes Sorel was one of the women whose physical and spiritual temperament marked her out for the position of the chosen *amoureuse*. She was beautiful, yet how many women were and are quite as beautiful who do not attain her destiny. She was more than beautiful, for her soul harmonised with her features. Nothing in her nature disappointed or deceived. The more she was known, the better she was loved. We must not gratuitously attribute to her selfish motives or vices to explain her success. Those who are without charm may employ such means to arrive at a result difficult for them to obtain otherwise. But let us be willing to concede, without prejudice, that some beings, especially favoured by nature, need only be born, grow, and appear before men to achieve their destiny. They do not go in search of glory or love; glory and love come to them, as if they were chosen beforehand from among all others. They have only to follow their inclination, like the springs flowing down the slope of a hill. Agnes had only to appear, to smile, and to triumph. Her docile acceptance of the opportunities offered her, her gentle sweetness were the only weapons she used to achieve victory.

But her destiny seems truly unique in one respect: this victory was not for her personal triumph nor directed selfishly to her individual, ephemeral glory. Her victory was that of France whom she served. Her grace, her goodness were instruments in the hands of a superior will involving interests infinitely beyond those of a mere woman, even though she were exceptionally beautiful. Agnes Sorel, in her fashion, saved France.

It might be assumed that, by a curious concurrence of circumstances, she was used unwittingly to this end, without her willing it, without her knowing it. But this is not so. She willed it, she knew it. She was not the supremely skilful promoter of an achievement, but she was more than merely the passive agent who made it possible. Her intelligence grasped the reasons for a course of action and served them with adroitness. She could not, of course, have carried out a task like this alone. But when once she understood what was expected of her, she performed her miracle calmly, and her miracle crowned that of Jeanne d'Arc. The same protecting hand which had guided the Maid, later guided the fair *amoureuse*. The work of restoring France would not have been complete without either. These two wonderful women should be placed on different, but not unequal planes, and glorified. The one with the sword, the other with a kiss, directed our national destiny.

Ah, I can see many of my readers knitting their brows in a frown or shrugging their shoulders sceptically. I greatly regret having to grieve or shock them, but one can only say what one believes, only believe what one knows, only know what is true according to the evidence of history. I do not intend here to depreciate the saint and to exalt the *amoureuse*. Their mysterious mission was the same, their means were different. They complemented each other without ever meeting, without knowing each other; they worked together in concerted action; their union was accomplished in the mind of a third person who understood how to employ them separately to attain the same end which she alone knew.

On reflection, is there not in every individual life and in the life of every nation one part that is divine, another that is human? We must act upon the world through God and through men. Heaven helps those who help themselves; the supernatural and the natural work in close collaboration. Here they are absolutely distinct and yet in perfect accord. When Jeanne d'Arc has achieved her mission by martyrdom, Agnes Sorel begins hers by love. The Maid in the white armour became merged in the air of France with the smoke that rose above her tragic martyrdom at the stake. Thereupon appeared the young girl, marvellous in her daring nudity. We have her image on the panel of the diptych of Antwerp, or as she appears in the work of an unknown painter at the Château de Mouchy, at once immodest and chaste. In the Antwerp picture, Jehan Fouquet did not hesitate to represent her as the Virgin Mary. The unknown painter shows her as a noble lady of sovereign degree, wearing a mantle lined with ermine, like a queen. A light, transparent veil falls from her radiant brow, her mantle is gathered around her perfect shoulders. Whether her hands hold a child or a book, they seem soft, perfumed like flowers, bending over the slender stalk of the frail wrist. The face has a delicacy that would discourage a less skilful brush, with its gently arching eyebrows; its nose slightly tilted; its small mouth; its fine, shell-like ears; its high, pearly brow. From the graciously yielding lace of her corselet her beautiful bosom is revealed to the admiring eyes, the breast firm, soft and of a milky whiteness, with its point rosy as the dawn. This bosom is of such dazzling beauty that it dispels all carnal thoughts, yet stirs, in the beholder, those hidden depths of emotion which we all conceal, for better or for worse. This bosom, the flower of the body, this bosom above all else gained for Agnes Sorel the titles of *"Belle des Belles," "plus belle," "Divine."*

Was she fair? We have our answer from Gabriel Boissy, the poet of the pines and of the cypresses of Provence who possessed a hair of the royal mistress. Her hair was chestnut with golden lights. It seemed fair at certain hours of the day when the sun lighted up its subdued brightness. The fairness of her complexion is characteristic of women inclined to be red-haired, but who stop in time before attaining that pronounced colouring.

Such was Agnes Sorel, who was born in July, 1409, at Fromenteau near Loches, in the parish of Villiers in Brenne, a province of Touraine. Her father was Jean Soreau, or Sorel, a squire, lord of Coudun and St. Géraut. Her mother was Catherine de Maignelais, a lady from Verneuil. Their coat-of-arms showed a green elder-tree upon a golden field.

Any one who has ever walked in the evening,

towards the close of September, in the country of the
Touraine knows that this is a delightful time of year
when the flowers, just about to die, send forth their
perfume in a despairing farewell. The coolness of the
evenings has already become more penetrating. It is
not yet autumn and it is no longer summer. This
season, hesitating and uncertain, has a little of both,
made up of melancholy and regret. There, on a road
well-known to me, the passer-by is overcome, almost
without being conscious of it, by an odour of overwhelming strength and sweetness. It is exhaled by the
fragile berries of an elder-tree near by, swaying in the
evening breeze. This same elder-tree in the coat-of-
arms of Agnes Sorel is a perfect symbol of her personality. Perhaps her charm and her dangerous quality
were hereditary. She carried these qualities to final perfection. She was the flowering and the supreme glory
of a family without great renown but of established
position, although it was only of the lesser nobility,
and of assured loyalty.

An orphan from her earliest youth, she was shel-
tered and brought up by an aunt, Madame de Maignelais, who loved her like her own daughter. The child's
destiny marked her out from the first. Alone in the
world, she had to draw out of herself the elements that

led to her success. Without wishing or even demanding it, she was distinguished and preferred, chosen
above others. Soon she aroused two contrary yet insep-
arable emotions, love and jealousy. Whoever is loved
must inevitably be hated. Because one is preferred, one
must be envied. The love which one inspires is more
desired than the fortune which one acquires. This is
because it is a mysterious force which no one can obtain
unless he possesses it in himself. It is a free gift of fate,
an undeserved favour; its unchallenged power is victorious against all attacks. Phryne before her judges
had only to reveal her charms to be pardoned. Hatch
the darkest plots, spread the blackest calumnies, set the
most artful snares . . . Agnes had only to unclose her
corselet and lower her languishing eyelids. That
bosom, that glance dissolved all useless words to noth-
ingness; love conquered hate. But neither love nor
hate will ever leave her in the course of her short life,
they will pursue her even beyond the grave; and because she was so greatly loved, Agnes Sorel will be
calumniated, sullied by the very persons who would
have adored her if they had only seen her once. But
all this is without importance in the final judgment
which must be passed upon her. She lived out her
whole destiny and that destiny was magnificent.

This love, this hate, stood by her side from her earliest years, like two inexorable guardians. Her aunt Maignelais secretly preferred Agnes to her own daughter Antoinette. Antoinette, secretly too, hated her cousin because of her mother's preference, however justified it was. Both girls were beautiful, but Agnes had more than beauty of features, she had that irradiation which comes from the soul. Her fair skin, her bright eyes, her perfect form would have been nothing without the air of calm and serenity emanating from her presence. If Antoinette wished to be loved, it was chiefly from pride. Agnes wished to be loved from necessity. She gave before she received and even demanded no more than to be received with kindness. The movement of her hand, the languor of her glance, her frank, undesigning words reassured her listener before convincing him, and without laying claim to anything she triumphed over all.

Along with this, she had a natural wit, quite free from any self-consciousness about the effect of her words. What a great man, Talleyrand de Périgord, said of his mother many years later, might be applied to Agnes—she wanted only to please and to lose what she gave in talk. But nothing with her was lost. She sowed love and she reaped the harvest quickly. Did she

LOCHES. SOUTHEAST SIDE

CHINON. THE CLOCK-TOWER

take note of her cousin's aversion? Did she feign not to see it? Did she hope to overcome it by sweetness and patience? In any event, she was always faithful to her and this fidelity later cost her her greatest sorrow, for the day was to come when this hate, with time as an accomplice, would triumph over her tenderness. Hate one day would vanquish love.

But before that hour, the last hour of her life, would arrive, she had to fulfil her destiny as a woman, an instrument of the higher destiny of the realm. Such beauty as hers is rare. Perfection is not for this world, is a common saying. Yet it was said and believed that in Agnes Sorel perfection was incarnate. Her fame passed beyond the limits of her province, it penetrated to the court which often stayed at Loches, at Chinon, or at Amboise. Charles VII knew the name of the woman he was to love long before he saw her, for before she could pass before his eyes, the young girl had still to complete her education and to travel a long way in preparation for her sudden ascent.

It was with a view to her future that her aunt found a place for her at the court of Isabelle of Lorraine; for it was the custom at that time to put young girls of good family in the service of great ladies as their companions. In return, their patronesses assumed the obligation of establishing their charges suitably in life.

A better choice could not have been made for either of them. Isabelle was the daughter of Charles I of Lorraine who, having no son born of his marriage with Margaret of Bavaria, caused the duchy of Lorraine to be declared a feminine fief, to the sole end that it should devolve upon his daughter in whom he had recognised a sovereign intelligence.

But another than he had also marked this distinguished young girl, and this other person was that woman "of great bearing," undoubtedly one of the supreme figures of that age, the King's mother-in-law, the Queen of Sicily, Yolande of Aragon by birth, later Yolande of Anjou. To her was due the victory over the English as well as the rise of France.

No one up to the present has rendered her full justice. Her name is mentioned, to be sure, but her secret rôle has not been sufficiently brought into the light, it has not been sufficiently glorified. I shall here apply to her the remark which I have often written before: whoever does not advertise himself must not count on others to undertake this task. To the people who understand how to make the grand gesture, to play the leading rôle in the drama, who from the first are marked out to attract the attention of the world, go its admiration and its homage. Later, when they are studied at close range, it often becomes apparent that they really were not so important as they gave themselves out to be. The eddy which they created around themselves prevented a clear view of others who, more modest or prouder (for disdain is the supreme form of pride), neglected to push themselves forward. The phrase which Cesare Borgia later pronounced is characteristic of all the successful climbers of all ages:

I make a noise, I am all the rage, there's news only about me.

Charles VII has been called "Charles the Well-Served." As always, this title has been accepted without looking farther into the cause for it. It is very certain that it was not his person which called forth devotion, nor was it his intelligence which aroused it. If he was not the stupid creature that he is often represented to be, still he had none of the royal genius of his son, Louis XI, none of the invincible fascination of his great ancestor, Louis IX. If he was well served, the reason is that close beside him watched a sovereign will, an intelligence of the first order. It was Yolande of Aragon, known also as Yolande of Anjou, his

mother-in-law, who exercised this will and this intelligence.

From the time when she had betrothed her daughter
Marie, at the age of ten, to the son of Charles VI and
Isabella of Bavaria, she held her protecting mantle over
this pair of children. In the future she will watch over
the kingdom of France, whose cause she will make
one with that of Anjou, thus preserving the interests
of her sons. From that time on, there stood always confronting the King's mother, who delivered France to
the enemy, ruining her own son and giving her daughter in marriage to the English prince so that he might
seize the crown of lilies—confronting her stood the
Angevin queen with the subtle mind, who seized and
held the threads of French statecraft.

At first it was through his young wife Marie that
she acted on the weak King, despoiled by his mother.
But soon the influence of the little queen no longer
sufficed. The English prince was crowned in France.
Now Charles abandoned himself to his fate, sunk deep
in debauchery. Yolande summoned to his side men
renowned in war, counsellors full of wisdom; one by
one she removed his grasping counsellors, his dissolute
mistresses. The situation did not become any the less
hopeless, however, for the "King of Bourges," as

Charles VII was now commonly called, took no interest in his kingdom. It was imperative, then, to rally with all possibly energy, the princes of France, sovereigns of their own domains and divided in opinion because self-interest alone guided them. Yolande therefore married her son René to Isabelle of Lorraine at Nancy, in 1420. This was an act of profound political wisdom on the part of the clever old queen. Up to that time, Charles I, Duke of Lorraine, had lent his support to the English cause; aid that was formidable for France. By this marriage, Lorraine was detached from the enemy and attached by the ties of blood to the Valois. But policy alone was not enough in this superstitious and mystic age. It was necessary to strike the imagination, to call God to aid and, in order to inspire men with courage, to make them believe that heaven was at last taking pity on their misery and lending an ear to their prayers. The hordes of the enemy were plundering the cities, setting fire to the villages, and torturing the terrified inhabitants. On every hand sorcerers and witches sprang up, professing themselves to be invested with divine powers and charged with the task of saving the realm. The blind faith accorded them by the people was not to be scorned as a means of relief. What was needed still more, however, was that these emissaries of God should be able to carry their mission to a successful end. Several were tested who disappointed all expectations. Then it was that in Lorraine, in the very province whose Duchess, Isabelle, was married to Yolande's son, René of Anjou, an inspired shepherdess, called Jeanne d'Arc, appeared. It may be well here to recall in a few words this strange story, so well-known but always new because of the miracle it embodies.

Jeanne was born on January 6th, 1412, at Domrémy, where she guarded her father's sheep. He was a peasant in easy circumstances, even wealthy for his position in life, according to popular report. Jeanne was devout and charitable, physically strong and well-built, gay, simple and wise. Like all the villagers, she heard the tales of the misery of her country, the pitiful state of her king, the destructive boldness of the English. In her direct, straightforward mind, where subtleties had no hold, she saw the situation clearly: the enemy was within the house, he must be put out, just as she did when, in guarding her sheep, a wolf came prowling in the neighbourhood. By dint of reflecting on these matters, she came to hear, in the solitude of her fields, voices from the trees. They told her they were the voices of St. Michael, St. Margaret, and St. Catherine enjoining her to go forth to save her country. "France, which was lost by a woman, must be saved by a virgin."

Her family, her companions surely laughed at her when she related these prodigies. But what power have men against the Idea which leads them? For three years Jeanne struggled against her inspiration. Then, one day she had her uncle conduct her to the commander of Vaucouleurs, the Sire de Baudricourt. She spoke to him sensibly and firmly, not as a visionary but as an agent of God, so assured in her persistence and simplicity that the rough captain was impressed by her. None the less, he dismissed the shepherdess, ridiculing her in order to discourage her. But it is certain that he must have reported the matter to his superiors and so the name of Jeanne came to the ears of the Duke of Lorraine, René, and through him to those of Yolande, mother-in-law of the King. She thought the matter over. We have said that a miraculous intervention was needed to restore confidence in the discouraged people, in the prince abandoned by his followers. Yet they still waited. Jeanne's father, too, was opposed to her mission, her friends jeered at her, the Sire de Baudricourt discouraged her.

"If I had had a hundred fathers and a hundred

mothers," she was to say later, "if I had been the daughter of the King, I should have gone forth none the less."

This admirable, instinctive assurance was equalled by her admirable, undivided desire to serve. She returned once more to the Commander of Vaucouleurs, who listened to her more attentively this time:

"I must go before the King," she repeated, "even if I must wear down my legs to the knees, because no one in the world, neither the King, nor duke, nor the daughter of the King of Scotland, nor any other can recover the kingdom of France, nor can any help be expected except through me. Surely I should rather spin by my mother's side, for this is not my chosen calling; but I must go and act because my Lord wishes me to do so."

Then it was, we may safely assert, that Baudricourt received orders from Chinon and agreed to conduct the shepherdess to the court, where she wished to go. It was a chance that must be risked and, after all, in the state of affairs then prevailing, what did they risk? She received a military outfit, a black jerkin, trunk-hose fastened by aglets, a short black tunic, a black hat, leggings with spurs, and a sword. It was the time when the siege of Orléans filled the realm with anguish, the time designated by the Maid for divine intervention whose instrument she declared herself to be. Baudricourt had her start forth by night and, with two men-at-arms and four servants on horseback, the little band set out to seek the king at Chinon.

Was a miracle needed? Was this not a miracle, then, appearing in this shepherdess with the clear glance, without fear? But they were interested only in practical miracles. That the young girl, urged on by instinctive patriotism, should have heard and understood the voices of her native Lorraine could happen without the assistance of any one; but, after that, if she were to accomplish her mission, human intervention must aid divine intervention. We are not belittling the rôle of Jeanne in recognising that she was aided by a worldly power, even as she was inspired by divine power. God chooses, men appoint the instrument. From the moment when she left her native village, Jeanne was guided by a protecting hand which smoothed the way for her mission. That hand was the hand of Yolande of Anjou. It was she who knew the King's weak spot, she who knew that, before all other conquests, must be achieved the conquest of this weak, shrinking spirit, mistrusting itself and all others. The old Queen of Sicily prompted the young girl about the reply she must make to inspire Charles with the consciousness of his part and to arouse his spirit, darkened by so many disastrous events. If he gave himself up to debauchery and refused to face the enemy, it was because he did not believe himself to be the son of France, since his own mother had treated him as a bastard. If the voice of a pure spirit assured him of his ancestry, he would at once have confidence in himself again, he would perhaps raise himself out of the muck, he would feel and know himself to be King, and then his people would follow him.

Jeanne is received with kindness; she has numerous secret conversations at her various halting-places. Gradually she is admitted into the secret which she has hitherto only known as a presentiment and divined. Her practical intelligence enters at once into the spirit of her rôle, the word which delivered Charles VII from his enchantment is pronounced by her:

I tell you from my Lord that you are the true heir of France and son of the King.

Undoubtedly this word has been whispered to her by the prompter behind the scenes. Forthwith the miracle is accomplished. But was he really heir of France and son of the King? Isabella, his mother, knew better than any one else and she asserted the contrary. But it was necessary that the people should have, against her testimony, the testimony of heaven proclaimed by the voice of the Maid. The assurance of the King's legitimacy rallied around him loyalties that had hesitated before. The divine law of the right of accession to the throne was recognised once more, the crown of France was duly reclaimed by the only being who had a right to it. So Jeanne, placed under the intelligent protection of Yolande and of Marie, the Queen, could not disappoint any hopes. We know of this alliance of the three women by the evidence of the Maid herself. She loved with a special tenderness the young wife of the King. She called her *"my Queen."* When the ladies of Luxemburg urged her to assume feminine garments, she replied:

"I am sorry to have to refuse you anything, but in France I would not have done this at the request of any one except my Queen." She knew well that to Marie as well as to Yolande, her mother, she owed the fact that she had been able to fulfil her mission. It was through them that she saved France.

When her rôle was accomplished, her two eminent friends abandoned her, proof sufficient that they never regarded the shepherdess as anything but an instru-

ment to play upon. There were more pressing prob-
lems to settle. Orléans was taken, but the whole kingdom remained to be conquered. This was merely an
episode in the drama. Jeanne did not drive out the
English, she gave the French the necessary courage to
drive them out. Though the King had been crowned
at Reims, he still continued to be the prey of his vices,
his favourites, his mistresses. With him, the beginning
had always to be made over again. He had to be
watched over like a child. The confidence with which
Jeanne had inspired him lasted only during the time of
a victory. But Yolande remained at her post as counsel-
lor. The saint had come, had conquered, had been delivered over to her enemies, was about to receive the
crown of martyrdom. She was no longer useful at
court. She was abandoned. All the more readily because there, too, she was thought to be a sorceress. As
such they had made use of her power. The old Queen
who had played upon her skilfully now had need of
other weapons to save the realm, still in the hands of
the invaders, and to direct her son-in-law whose weakness kept his party in constant peril of defeat
(1430).

Charles I of Lorraine died in 1431. Isabelle and René
ascended the throne of Lorraine. He was that good

RENÉ OF ANJOU: "GOOD KING RENÉ"
Bibliothèque Nationale

King René whose gracious memory is preserved in legend. A poet, a painter, a scholar, Provence looked on him as its chosen, revered master. Isabelle, his wife, was as delightful a being as he, but with a spirit of another temper. Gay and energetic, she loved luxury and finery. As old as Agnes Sorel, adoring her like all who lived near her, she did not now part from her. At Nancy, where the court of Lorraine resided, there was a succession of banquets and festivals, and the *demoiselle* Sorel there developed her beauty and her wit.

But hardly had the good King René assumed the crown of Lorraine when his cousin, Antoine de Vaudémont, disputed it. They engaged in war and René was made prisoner on the field of Bulgnéville.

"Spare my life and let me be ransomed for a good, round sum," he said as he put up his sword.

Yolande at once advised her daughter-in-law to summon the council of Lorraine, to rally her army at Nancy and to demand aid from the King of France (1432). It was to seek out Charles at Chinon that Isabelle set out on her errand, with all her brilliant train and attended by her beloved companion, Agnes Sorel.

The story goes that as soon as he saw her, Charles

stood abashed and amazed. We have said that he was
a lover and admirer of women, and this young girl,
fair and smiling, must needs have made a great impression on him. But she was prudent and did not at
once yield to this homage. Isabelle, when her mission
was completed and she had obtained the support which
she had asked, planned to depart and to take with her
her faithful attendant. The King would not consent to
this, his heart had been captured. Queen Marie herself, too, thought Agnes charming; the old Queen of
Sicily, Yolande, realised at once the advantage which
she could gain through the influence of this gentle,
intelligent young woman, submissive to her views, delivered into her hands as an instrument of her policy,
as Jeanne had been of her purpose. Isabelle undoubtedly realised the import of these far-reaching designs,
sorrowfully consented to separate from her friend, and
departed without her. It has been said that, in order
to make her entrance into the Queen's service seem
plausible in the malicious eyes of the court, the young
girl feigned an illness which prevented her return to
Lorraine with her mistress. But there was no need of
a pretext. The King desired her. In this desire Yolande
saw all that she could hope for in the way of attaining
a higher object. So Isabelle could only yield, the more

so as she was very soon struggling with difficulties which left her no time to regret this separation.

Then, too, it was not an age of useless sentimentality and childish lamentations. The fifteenth century was a violent, realistic age. Passions were expressed brutally, clashing interests defended themselves forcibly. Agnes was useful, Agnes must remain behind. Isabelle, whose husband was still a prisoner, was now the lieutenant-general of her domain. When the brother of René of Anjou, Louis III, Count of Provence, died at this time, he left him his estates, while Jeanne de Duras bequeathed to him Naples, Sicily and Jerusalem. Forced to defend her interests, Isabelle embarked from Marseilles and remained in Italy seven years (1435).

Agnes belonged to the King of France.

CHAPTER II
The King's Awakening

CHAPTER II

The King's Awakening

WHO was this King and what was he like to whom fell this flower of feminine sweetness and tenderness, this fair beauty who was able to unite unswerving sincerity to the larger interests unquestionably at stake, who became an instrument of statecraft in the hands of the cunning queen, his mother-in-law, while she remained ever an object of love to the King whom she was about to delight? Who and what was this Charles VII, then?

It is the year 1435. Jeanne d'Arc had inspired him with confidence in himself, but not with a desire for personal action. He knew now that he was the legitimate master of France, but he did not make others feel it. He took pride in his title, but he did not yet know that he must assume its responsibilities. At the time when Agnes entered his life, he was still, in spite of his coronation at Reims, "the king of Bourges." The flaming path of the Maid, her victory, her suffering, were only the initial letter, illumined in gold and red, of the great national impulse of which she was the point of departure. To-day Jeanne has become the saint of France. In her own day, she was not so hailed. Her activities ended at the stake at Rouen; the court accepted the verdict of the church; they had done well to burn the sorceress. When this had been settled, they no longer thought of her. The King, occupied with his pleasures, trusted his captains to carry on the war, his mother-in-law to carry on the political game.

There is a story told of La Hire, one of the King's bravest military leaders, who later had the honour of appearing in his card games—supreme mockery of glory!—La Hire, arriving one day, all covered with sweat, at Chinon, to receive orders from the King, found him occupied in rehearsing a ballet in which he was to take part. Then the fiery Captain cried: "Sire, never before has a prince been seen or heard of who lost his state so gaily."

It was this same La Hire, a paragon of courage and honour, who said one day to Pothon, his companion in arms: "Comrade, to-morrow we shall fight the English who have so many archers that their arrows will darken the light of the sun."

To this Pothon replied: "That is good news, then we shall fight in the shade."

A fine example of French humour this! Its echo was heard in the trenches of Artois and on the fields

CHARLES VII, KING OF FRANCE, THE VICTORIOUS

From the Portrait by Jehan Fouquet in the Louvre

of the Marne, with its vigorous phrases, its bold gestures, its smiling heroism, its simple faith.

Another story is told of La Hire, that splendid servant to glory. Before engaging in battle, he knelt and prayed to God: "Lord, I pray you that you will to-day do for La Hire as much as you would wish La Hire to do for you, if he were God and you were La Hire."

These fine soldiers whom Jeanne, the young Maid, ardent and wise, had trained for a war that was to restore the kingdom, these fine soldiers deserved a better king than the one for whom they gave their lives so joyfully.

The authentic portraits of Charles VII show that he was thin and dark like his mother Isabella, of unsteady gait and with weak, knock-kneed legs that explain why he preferred to wear long robes at a time when tight-fitting garments clearly defined the lines of the figure. Inconstant, mistrustful, envious, he was full of "mutability, mistrust and envy," or rather timorous as a result of his tortured, tragic childhood. His father, or he who was called his father, Charles VI, was mad. His mother Isabella was mad, too, after her fashion, mad for her pleasures and her body. There was much talk in Paris in the year 1403 and the following years of the orgies at the Hôtels St. Paul,

Nesles, and the Petit Musc. It was after one of these nights of debauchery and love that Louis, Duke of Orléans, the Queen's lover, was assassinated by John the Fearless, Duke of Burgundy.

Charles had seen his older brothers all die before him; he alone remained, puny and scorned, to assume the heavy responsibility of royal power, still merely imaginary, with which his mother was trafficking with the English.

On the night between April 28th to April 29th, 1418, while the tocsin sounded for the massacre of the Armagnacs, the mayor of Paris, Tanneguy du Chatel, came to take him from his bed, as a precious symbol of phantom authority destined one day to rally around him a nation betrayed and rent asunder. He wrapped him in his mantle, while the child lay trembling in his bed at the Hôtel St. Paul, awaiting his death. From there, the mayor bore him to the Bastille, then to Bourges, then to Poitiers.

It was in the following year, 1419, on the first of September, on the bridge at Montereau, that his people, without his knowledge and in accord with the Orléans faction, in reprisal for the murder of Duke Louis, assassinated John, Duke of Burgundy, his murderer.

LOUIS, DUKE OF ORLÉANS
From a Contemporary Portrait in a Private Collection

On another occasion, when he was at La Rochelle, the ceiling of the room where he was standing fell, killing several of his friends. It was a miracle that he escaped alive.

All these tragic events and their attendant emotions shook his nerves, already weak because of his terrible heredity, and made him a man of "mutable" temperament; that is to say, they made him shrinking, uncertain, full of fear, full of the morbid timidity of which his subjects complained. It was said that he could not endure being looked at, especially by those whom he did not know. He was at once put out of countenance, being always in great terror of assassination.

He had, however, an exceptionally fine, strong memory. He loved history and it was he who later restored the records of the Great Chronicles of St. Denis. He was a good Latin scholar, though it remains a cause of wonder where and when he found time to study, little though it might be, in the anarchy of that epoch; and when he was not trembling with fear his judgment was sound. His voice is said to have been agreeable, like his son's, so that it has been called "a siren" voice. This added greatly to his powers of captivation. The chronicler, Jean Chastelain, ends his ac-

count of him as follows: "Nevertheless he had many
virtues by which, along with the assistance of various
great lords and, above all by the help of God, he attained a brilliant and glorious destiny."

We have said that if divine Providence, taking
visible form in Jeanne, watched over the destiny of
France through her, a human providence watched
over the accomplishment of its mysterious designs.
Yolande of Anjou understood all the resources and
all the weaknesses of this variable, shrinking nature.
Having succeeded so well in promoting the martial
achievement of the Maid of Lorraine she must now
succeed equally well in assisting the work of statecraft of the young girl from Touraine whom she thrust
into the arms of Charles, at once to delight and to direct him.

The King had married Yolande's daughter, Marie,
sister of René, when he was scarcely twelve years old,
she only ten. These marriages between children, which
seemed so charming, had deplorable results from the
erotic and physical point of view. The premature delights of love enervated and exhausted, wore out or
instilled irresistible desires and evil habits in certain
temperaments. Added to this was a dangerous heredity, that of his mad father and of Isabella, the un-

bridled, whose lovers were unnumbered and whose loose habits, acquired under the influence of a dissolute court, added to the misfortunes of the realm. This serves to explain the King's inclination towards pleasure, his constant need of surrounding himself with men and women favourites with whom he gave himself over to the basest orgies.

There is at Amboise, at some distance from the château, a little fifteenth century house with turrets, gables and dovecots, called the Pages' House, or *les Gironnets*. On the side of the steep cliff, looking down upon the Loire, it lies outside the château but is connected with it by a road which joined the round-way. *Les Gironnets* was Charles VII's pleasure house, his bachelor's quarters, his Folly, if one may employ this term in anticipation of a later day. There he retired secretly at evening, trailing his long robes over the narrow path. The lofty hall with its great sculptured fireplace preserves the memory of those equivocal hours, where, with Cadart, the physician; Louvet, the financier, and his daughter Jeanne; Pierre de Giac, squire of Auvergne; Le Camus de Beaulieu and Georges de la Trémoille, he gave himself over to excesses, so far as his powers, weakened by his dubious heredity, permitted.

Then at last, when things had gone beyond all bounds, Arthur, Earl of Richmond, of the ruling house of Brittany, high Constable of France, commonly known as "the judge," with the connivance of the old Queen of Sicily, arose like the Commander in Shakespeare's drama and, quick of decision, swift of execution, got rid of the King's favourites of a day. One by one they disappeared, one struck down by a poniard by an unknown hand, another tossed into the river in a sack, regretted not even by the King himself.

The time had come to surround the prince, worn out by his excesses, with wise, strong counsellors who would complete the work begun by the heroic Maid. To force them upon him without more ado was not to be contemplated. Charles would always escape from their influence, especially if he felt that it was a wise, just influence; still elusive, he would escape it. Pleasure must be the artful means to employ if one wished to succeed in holding him to his duties. Love must be the way of leading the prince back to the lofty mission implied in his title.

Agnes Sorel was the person chosen by the subtle old queen to impose on him her guiding will and protecting spirit.

No little self-abnegation was required of the damsel chosen for this rôle. Agnes was charming, delicate, and already a cherished favourite at the court of Lorraine. She must leave the court of Nancy, celebrated for its luxury and elegance, the intelligent companionship of Isabelle of Lorraine and of René, the good, the artist King, to dwell at the court of France, officially attached to the service of Queen Marie, officiously to the King whose scandalous life was a matter of common report. At this time he was still "the pauper king." His poverty scarcely permitted him to dress and support himself, his wife and his son, the Dauphin, in fitting manner. The account-books of the time make this lamentable situation clear. Fish appeared on the royal table more than meat. Once, it is related, when the court arrived at the château of Amboise, they had to put waxed paper in place of the broken panes of glass through which the bitter winter winds penetrated. When the tradesmen came to ask for payments long overdue, the King humbly begged for another postponement. Naturally the satirists of the period did not fail to scoff at this penury and the ballads about Charles VII were frankly derisive of the royal state.

> One day La Hire and le Pothon
> Came to visit him at a banquet—

They had only a mutton tail
And two chickens—and that was all.

Certain apologists of Agnes Sorel see in her willingness to accept the favour of so destitute a lover proof of a splendid disinterestedness. She deserves some credit for this assuredly, but it must not be exaggerated. She was well aware that the King's poverty was only temporary. The initial victory must inevitably be concluded and concluded through her, if she remained submissive not to the commands but to the adroit suggestions of her benefactor and manager, Yolande. It would be equally unjust and false to see in this young woman, of whom such valuable and special services were demanded, either covetousness or venality, against which her nature protected her. Finally, we know from the records of expenses of Isabelle of Lorraine that Agnes, at the court of the King of France, still received subsidies from her former mistress and friend. One of the entries reads: "Ten *livres* of the currency of Tours [1] for the salary of Agnes Sorel, one of the young ladies, for accompanying her."

Then, too, Charles VII, though he lacked so many royal qualities, was generous by nature. He loved to give. "He was a recluse," people said, but he was lavish

[1] A *livre* of Tours was worth about ten pence.

in his rewards when he could afford it, especially to those whom he loved. Agnes knew, then, that as soon as the kingdom was freed of the enemy she would be one of the first to be loaded with favours. She knew this but, disinterested as she was by nature, she probably did not give it a thought.

Beyond this hope for the future, did she love the King with a great, tender, passionate love? It would appear so, for she always remained faithful to him. We have seen that Charles was not handsome, but he had a fine voice. He was weak, in want, unfortunate. Her woman's heart was touched by her lover's need of protection and consolation. He, whose mother had been unworthy and full of hate towards him, whose wife had been too young to aid and sustain him, whose men and women favourites had only shared his pleasures, obedient to his caprices, now for the first time found a woman worthy of the name. What a light her smiling gentleness must have shed on his life, so dark and violent up to this moment! What peace her goodness must have brought to his nerves strained to the breaking-point by pleasure and by fear! Her intelligence and her judgment, always ready with good counsel, must have brought relaxation and a new strength to his yielding will. For the first time a feeling must have sprung up in him which life had hitherto denied him: confidence. In wooing Agnes, he sought a mistress as much as a friend. Her beautiful hands on his tortured brow drove away the fears lurking there. He leaned upon her fair bosom with a lover's delight, but perhaps also like a child who had never felt a mother's tenderness.

Agnes "the peaceful" she is called in the old chronicles. Peaceful and loyal. Her long eyelids, when lowered, cast a pensive shadow that stirred men's dreams. She is Sorel, she is Soreau, and the elder-tree of her coat-of-arms is a symbol of the spiritual perfume exhaled from her, the perfume of late summer evenings in the quiet, peaceful country.

So endowed, so prepared, guided by destiny, supported by the clear-sighted will of the old queen, Agnes went to fulfil her mission. Jeanne the Maid, in raising her blessed oriflamme on high, had waved these prophetic words above her head: *"De par le roy du ciel!"* ("In the name of the King of Heaven!") Agnes, a creature of this world and a woman made for love, follows that woful figure, bearing no weapons, but quite disarmed; wearing no casket of steel, but veiled in white; not clothed in chastity and purity, but revealing her perfect form and wonderful bosom. She says: "I am Agnes. Long live France!" And in doing so, Agnes was about to complete the miracle of Jeanne —Charles, the little "King of Bourges," was about to become Charles the Victorious.

Here I may perhaps be allowed to refer to a page of Brantôme to justify my words: "Assuredly, while there are many men valiant by nature, women incite them to courageous deeds still more; and when they become weary and indifferent, women restore and inspire their spirit. We have a very beautiful example of this in the fair Agnes. When she saw that the King, Charles VII, greatly enamoured of her, cared only to make love to her and, feeble and mean-spirited, paid no heed to his kingdom, she related to him one day that, when she was still a young girl, an astrologer had foretold that she would be loved and cared for by one of the bravest and most valiant kings of Christendom. When the King first did her the honour of loving her, she thought that he must be this valiant king who had been foretold to her; but seeing him now, so slothful and so heedless of the affairs of his realm, she realised clearly that she had been mistaken and that this courageous king, predestined for her, was not he, but the King of England who fought so magnificently and captured so many fine cities beneath the French King's nose. 'So,' she concluded her speech to the King, 'I must go to find him because it must be he of whom the astrologer spoke to me.' These words pierced the King's heart so sharply that he began to weep. Then, plucking up courage and abandoning the pleasures of the chase and his gardens, he took the bit in his teeth so successfully that, by good fortune and his daring, he drove the English from his kingdom."

The tradition of Agnes' influence on Charles is widespread. There is a portrait of the royal favourite in existence, presented by her to her friend Guillaume Gouffier and handed down in his family, on which King Francis I has inscribed these verses to accompany the delightful image:

> Gentille Agnès, plus de los en mérite
> La cause étant la France recouvrer,
> Que ce que peut dedans un cloitre ouvrer,
> Close nonnain ou bien dévot hermite.

That is to say, the love of this beautiful woman did more for the royal cause, combined with the cause of her country, than all the prayers of the pious men and women shut up in their convents, since love is the generator of great achievements. This knightly king was surely an authority in this matter and we must accept his verdict.

There are two sources in the search for historic truth: documents properly so called, emanating from the individuals themselves; the impressions spontaneously produced by them on their contemporaries and handed down. I say "spontaneously" because, after too carefully considered judgments are passed, we merely come upon mocking apologies or absurd disparagement.

Immediate friends or enemies have no value as witnesses any more than those whom they have influenced. But the others, all the others who are nameless and who have no interest in demolishing or exalting the character before them, those who judge a cause by its effect, without lingering over individual conscientious scruples or unimportant details, are valuable witnesses. When a battle has been won, we ask where is the general? He is the one glorified because he bore the responsibility.

These facts are undeniable: the English began their retreat after the appearance of Jeanne d'Arc. The King was aroused out of his cowardly torpor by the influence of his fair favourite.

> Sire, take up your arms and arm your warriors,
> Deliver your subjects, drive from your land
> Your ancient foe. Then I, most fortunate

In possessing the favour of a magnanimous king,
As the well-beloved of a victorious king,
I shall be forever esteemed by the French people.
If honour cannot call you away from love
You can at least acquaint love with honour.

So she spoke to him, and her loving voice
Struck a spark of courage in the amiable king.

These verses are by Antoine du Baïf, a sixteenth century poet who was inspired by a tradition still fresh in the minds of his contemporaries. They agree with those of Francis I in attesting the patriotic feeling of Agnes Sorel in which people believed at this time, though it was very near her own. They bear witness to her inspiring influence on her lover, sunk in slumber until her coming.

There can be no doubt that the honour for this achievement is due to Yolande of Anjou who understood how to make use of her precious weapon. None the less, the old Queen of Sicily, without this young, intelligent, sensitive woman to aid her, would not have been able to influence the restive mind of her son-in-law. With the King, delight must accompany good counsel. He had to be beguiled in order to be guided. He must have love and beauty. With these, Agnes played her game and won. It meant victory for France.

So her device should have another word to complete it and it was Voltaire who made it read so:

I am Agnes. Long live France!
I am Agnes. Long live France and Love . . . !

§   §

And what was the Queen's part in all this drama—Queen Marie of Anjou, daughter of Yolande, who presented her son-in-law with a mistress of her own choosing to serve her policies according to her own wish?

We must be careful not to judge the past according to our present standards. All the errors of historical evaluation, all the absurd judgments passed on the personages of former times can be laid to this tendency. And yet, to speak of our "standards" is perhaps saying too much . . . ! Have they changed so greatly, after all? What has changed has been the outward appearance. Not virtue, but hypocrisy has increased. We have to-day, just as in times past, our leaders of state who have their fair favourites. They cost quite as much and they are far more numerous. Did a king load his mistress with favours in times past? Every deputy now has his, and that makes how many favourites in the republic? We do not know their names, or rather we will not remember their names in the future; they do not display their wealth in the bright light of day before the world. The money swallowed up by them goes for motor cars and necklaces. In the past an official mistress erected castles which remain to this day, restored to the national inheritance, to enrich it and inform us about the arts which transcend morals.

What are we to think of the Queen of Sicily who assisted her son-in-law in deceiving her daughter? It was imperative to drive "the English out of France." They had become so deeply rooted there in the last one hundred years that military action alone, no matter how admirably conducted, was not enough. Diplomatic action, too, steadily adhered to, was required in this crisis. The enemy held Paris, Normandy, la Guyenne. He had formed firm alliances with the great lords of France which must be dissolved. The character of Charles, changeable, fickle, easily influenced, "mutable," was well understood. Marie of Anjou had no hold of any sort on her husband. He remained attached to her and had children by her to safeguard the succession to the throne. She loved and respected him.

"He is my lord, he has authority over all my actions and I over none," she was accustomed to say.

A Flemish chronicler in the pay of the Duke of Burgundy, Georges Chastellain, felt that he must present Queen Marie in the attitude of one to be pitied and suffering. To keep the peace, according to him, she was forced to accept all this: "to see her rival walk beside her and remain near her every day, to have her household in the King's palace, to enjoy the company and all the gatherings of the lords and the nobility, to appear before her, to possess more beautiful bedclothes, better rings and jewels, enjoy a better table and better everything. And with all this she must not only put up, but rather make it seem a pleasure."

One can scarcely agree that Marie needed so much pity when one recalls the wildly licentious life of Duke Philip of Burgundy, Georges Chastellain's master, who kept twenty-four concubines and yet rendered honour to his own wife. It is doing an injury to Queen Marie of Anjou, a character of a different temper, whose psychology was worthy of her mother. The reasons for her slight influence on the King were many. The principal one was undoubtedly their too early marriage, which had quickly exhausted the adolescent prince; another lay in the character of the Queen herself, in which love was not the dominant nor most exacting quality.

At the Louvre there is a bust of this queen, wife of Charles VII, mother of Louis XI. Beneath its archaic forms, her character appears in definite outline. She has a long face, eyelids heavy and lowered, a large, drooping nose, a sly mouth and a large, thoughtful brow. She looks like one endowed with the gift of prophecy. From it we can understand that her clear judgment could foresee and provide against events. She loved money exceedingly and amassed it with cunning, secretly acquiring a fortune. Very intelligent, reared by her mother Yolande by the side of her brother René, the most scholarly prince of his age, a superior woman, she seems to have had, like her son Louis who resembled her in so many qualities, a definite vision of reality, an instinctive feeling for its demands. She established a perfect ménage with Charles. Neither the official nor the officious historians tell of any disagreement between them. Before being a wife, she was a queen.

The gift of prophecy which her contemporaries attribute to her was simply her perfect understanding of her position, of her age, of her environment, of herself and of the necessities to which she must submit. She soon understood the dissolute temperament of Charles and knew that she alone could not satisfy him.

QUEEN MARIE OF ANJOU
Wife of Charles VII and Friend of Agnes Sorel
Cabinet des Estampes
Bibliothèque Nationale

To check his early sensual excesses, which put him at the mercy of chance favourites of evil counsel, he needed a woman capable of satisfying him and of advising him. Her mother's choice seemed perfect to her. Submissive to suggestion, good, loyal, gentle, Agnes would be the husband's friend without being the wife's enemy. She would be his adviser without becoming his traducer. She would be the soft voice which could give expression to the most serious counsels. Perfect accord would reign not only in the royal household, but in the immediate circle around them. Marie loved Agnes as she had loved Jeanne d'Arc, both as useful instruments to achieve the national rise to power, the most important, the only important, business of the moment.

In this respect their conduct was in harmony with their epoch. There is no age in which religion was more powerful and less rigorous in its commands. Is this a contradiction? No, it was all a matter of policy. Concubines were received and made use of by the church which closed its eyes to their presence. Bastards were recognised and honoured. Philip of Burgundy who had twenty-four mistresses had fifteen illegitimate children by them.

"There are two kinds of love," said a writer of the

fourteenth century, "love within marriage, or love that is duty, and free love, or love by favour."

It is clear that often marriages of this sort were unsuitable, demanded solely by the interests of the state. A prince would marry a princess as a pledge of political alliance for him, a pledge of peace for the people. Charles by his alliance with Marie of Anjou acquired this province and the influence and power of the great lords of Anjou were added to his own. Yolande, to protect her own interests in her own states, worked out her ingenious combinations to save France which served her as a shield in her struggle to hold her possessions. Could more be demanded of a husband than respect for the partner of his policies who was not the partner of his love as well? Could he be deprived of Love by favour? Surely not. Provided that the mistress chosen by the King for this office was faithful, decent, loyal, and good, that was all that was required of her. If, in addition, she served imperative political ends, she would be recognised and acclaimed by all. On this account, no authoritative voice was raised against Agnes. Only Pope Pius II, who was angry at the King of France because of the Pragmatic Sanction, spoke with rancour of the favourite of whose influence over Charles he was well informed.

Monstrelet, an historian by no means above suspicion, writes only these simple words about Agnes: "There are various judgments about her." Unanimous commendation is not achieved in this world. Not to have suffered more disparagement is in itself a patent of virtue.

Agnes loved Charles alone and everything leads to the belief that she loved him sincerely. Her love was publicly accepted, since her children were acknowledged; it was approved, it was useful. She had her place at court; her presence was noted, her beauty was admired, her intellect was praised. "And her speech was so far beyond that of other women that she was regarded as a prodigy."

Her counsels were excellent; they emanated from one higher than she, to be sure, but she supported them with her native good sense and her good heart. A kiss sealed the agreements of state, hastened the necessary decisions. For this reason the King, madly in love with her who has been called the Fairest of the Fair, *"la douce, la suave amie,"* was obedient to her suggestions.

§   §

The love between Agnes and Charles began, as we have said, with the visit of Isabelle of Lorraine to the court at Chinon.

Chinon, situated at the border of the Vienne, was an old feudal castle surrounded by formidable towers, one of which still raises its challenging walls. It stood in all its vigorous splendour at that time, dominating the river above which it rose and the city which it protected. Its vast halls, still called the "old building," had a severe aspect which was not softened by the meagre state in which the court lived at this unhappy period. Charles was not yet master of his kingdom, he was only its conqueror. The King established his mistress in a building near the castle called the Roberdeau manor-house. It is reported that he went to pay his secret visits to her by way of dark underground tunnels. There is a tradition, too, still current, that when the King went to hunt, he shut up his mistress in a great tower which still exists. Was this because of jealousy, or perhaps rather to preserve the secret of this new love still so tender that indiscreet glances might have withered its delicious bloom?

However this may be, it was in this old castle where he lived with his rough captains, that this bright, warm ray of sunlight fell upon the morose king. The young girl's youth, her beauty and her tenderness seemed a promise of better days and her love like an annunciation that France, long rebellious to her legitimate king, was now at last about to accept him.

Agnes soon became the mother of her first daughter, Charlotte, born in 1433, acknowledged by the King as a daughter of France. On this occasion he presented the damsel of Fromenteau with the castle of Beauté from which she took the name that so well befitted her. It was not a castle in the proper sense of the word, but a delightful manor or country seat, situated at the edge of the forest of Vincennes, to the right of Nogent, commanding a view of the valley of the Marne. It was Charles V who had built it and Christine de Pisan, a woman poet of the time, wrote this comment about this celebrated spot: *"Beauté, which is a very remarkable domain."*

This country place with the Hôtel St. Paul at Paris were the favourite residences of the king called "the Wise." Many of his official documents are dated from the *"Chatel de Beauté-sur-Marne emprès le bois de Vincennes."* There he received in solemn state the Emperor Charles IV and there he passed away on September 16, 1380.

After the death of Charles V the villa was left deserted. No king came to live there, but lords of high degree were set over it to guard it, such as Bureau de la Rivière or the Count de Nevers. The *"Journal d'un Bourgeois de Paris"* calls it "the most beautiful and attractive castle and the most finely situated in all the Ile-de-France."

It consisted of a tower of three storeys, terminating in a platform. In each storey there was one large room, the first of which was called the chamber of the Evangelists, probably because of its decorations. Besides this tower there was the main building, containing one large chamber and two galleries looking upon a wonderful fountain, called the Fountain of Beauty. There the fairest woman of the realm must have watched her image, a lily bending over the watery mirror that reflected her beauty. There she smiled at her rare fortune, to be the beloved of the King and through him serving France, now awakened from a long torpor.

The birth of her first daughter, recognised as a sister of the Dauphin, placed Agnes in the rank of royal favourites. Thenceforward she shared the life of the court and attended the King and the Queen in their public and private lives; she became a channel of the King's favours and the silent collaborator of those who were striving to work towards the rebirth of the nation, grievously wounded.

§   §

The climb upward was difficult and rough. In reading at this long distance these simple words, "Charles VII reconquered his kingdom from the English," we sum up too briefly the enormous work of reconstruction devolving upon a king who scarcely seemed equal to his mission. It is usual, too, in crediting Jeanne d'Arc with the full, magnificent responsibility for the victory, to forget how brief was her appearance, how episodic her activity at the end of a long struggle, the last years of which were the most difficult to sustain. If it had only been a matter of "driving the English out of France," the task would have been, if not easy, at least simplified. But there was another conquest to be made, that of the great vassals who, looking only to their own interests, had supported the invader. One has only to recall that the Treaty of Brétigny of October fourteenth had given to the English Guines, Ponthieu, Poitou, Saintonge, Angoumois, Limousin, Périgord, Agenois, Quercy, Rouergue, Bigorre. It was half his kingdom, which King John had to sacrifice to regain his liberty. The Treaty of Troyes in May, 1420, signed

by Isabella and the Duke of Burgundy, had been no
less draconian. The marriage of the Princess Catherine,
daughter of Charles VI and Isabella, to the King of
England, Henvy V, had abolished the Salic Law that
excluded women from the throne and gave the crown
to their son, Henry VI. So, after the assassination of
the Duke of Burgundy at Montereau in reprisal for
the assassination of the Duke of Orléans at Paris, the
cause of King Charles VII seemed lost. Disinherited
by the will of his father, Charles VI, disavowed by his
mother, deserted by his great vassals, the authority of
the prince did not extend beyond Amboise and
Chinon. When Henry V of England was acclaimed
King of France at Notre-Dame, the poor Dauphin in
the solitude of Touraine was attended by only seventeen knights. His troops were composed of foreign adventurers, gathered from everywhere, Gascons, Bret-
ons, Lombards, and Scotch, under the command of
rough captains such as La Hire, Xaintrailles, Stewart,
Darnley, and Dunois, Bastard of Orléans. The great
lords, the great feudal heads had to be won over by
diplomacy and endless patience.

Then it was that the secret rôle of the royal favourite, led by a practised hand through tortuous ways, became evident. Their first concern was to detach from

England her fiery ally, the Duke of Burgundy, rendered well-nigh irreconcilable because of the murder of
his father by Charles VII, or at any rate by his devoted
followers. This was the crux of the situation. Since
Yolande exercised considerable influence over the
Duke, she undertook to win him over, trusting Agnes
to achieve with her lover the same work of reconciliation. The Duke must be made to forget his vengeance
or to feel that it had been sufficiently satisfied; the
King must remove the chiefs of his armies who had
served his interests when he was deserted by all others.
There was Tanneguy du Chatel, so loyal but so brutal,
who had himself struck the Duke down at Montereau.
There was his accomplice, Dunois. It was hard necessity that forced the prince to this ingratitude because
of the demands of diplomacy. Henceforward the rôle
of his old-time faithful servitors was finished; they
must give way to new counsellors, less brave perhaps,
more adroit, less rough and blustering. They must
even, to facilitate the work of reconciliation and ab-
solve the King, assume sole responsibility for the crime
at Montereau. It was a work of slow, gradual suggestion that Agnes must accomplish, under cover of her
love, substituting new faces for old. If the Duke of
Burgundy would lend his support to the restoration

of the French kingdom, victory was certain. The war had been begun under the Burgundian standard; it must be concluded under the same standard. Yolande, Agnes, the Duchess of Bourbon, sister of Duke Philip, assumed the burden of reconciliation.

It was in regard to this action, well-known among her contemporaries, that a prelate of that time, the bishop of Thérouine, called the Lady of Beauty "the new Herodias." It was she who influenced the men who were needed at this juncture, who removed the others with a smile which left no room for rancour. This was why, in addition to her charm, she held the King, her lover, captive through all her fleeting life, leaving behind her only a shining wake of beauty and kindnesses.

§   §

In another connection, Charles showed that he understood the art of fostering advantageous alliances. The Scotch had always been his faithful servitors and he always had near him, to protect his person, a Scotch guard. In recognition of these services and to seal the accord with these hereditary enemies of England, he arranged to marry his son, the Dauphin, to the daughter of James II of Scotland in 1436.

PHILIP, DUKE OF BURGUNDY
From a Contemporary Portrait in a Private Collection

This marriage must be celebrated with a brilliance which would proclaim to the eyes of the world that France was reborn. The King's poverty made him an object of ridicule among his enemies. At that time, as in ours, pomp and luxury were necessary to instil confidence in partisans who were still hesitating and fear in dissenters. Agnes gave the King the idea of this reception in honour of the little princess. The programme was arranged according to her taste.

This marriage was the first manifestation of princely splendour seen in France for many years, the first since Isabella, the mother of Charles, had come to France as a bride. After Agnes, Margaret of Scotland now appeared as a second ray of hope shining in a sky that was slowly clearing.

"On a great barge attended by three galleys and six barks, escorted by the French fleet, the young princess disembarked at La Rochelle. There she was received with affectionate welcome. Her passage through the country was attended by a succession of festivals and entertainments. As the treasury was empty, the customary tournaments were omitted, but the entrance into the city of Tours of the fair girl, mounted on a white mare, was enchanting. She stopped before the cathedral of St. Gatien to make her devotions there and advanced to Montils, where the King and the Queen received her. The Princess was twelve, the Dauphin fourteen years old. He looked handsome in his costume of Persian velvet, in a design of leaves embroidered in gold. She was dressed in the fashion of her country. They embraced and went to play in the garden. They were married soon after, but their union was not consummated until later at Gien."

Agnes could not be present at this wedding, as she was expecting a child soon. Étienne Chevalier, her friend and one of the new counsellors whom she had given to the king, was charged to remain near her and to inform the King as soon as she was delivered. The child was born soon after; it was again a girl and was named Marie. The King, who surrounded his favourite with every attention, acknowledged this child, too, and bestowed on the mother the castle of Bois-Trousseau near Bourges. The Queen, who was herself pregnant and soon after gave birth to a prince, became the godmother of the little girl who bore her name. Marie of France was reared at the castle of Taillebourg by Prégent de Coëtivy, Admiral of France. This fact and others show how different were the ideas of those days from ours to-day and how dangerous it is to confuse

ARRIVÉE DE LA DAUPHINE.

Marguerite d'Écosse

MARGARET OF SCOTLAND

Daughter of James II and Wife of the Dauphin

Cabinet des Estampes
Bibliothèque Nationale

them. Of Dunois, Bastard of Orléans, his wife, Valentine of Milan, who adored him, said that "he had been captured by her." Queen Marie occupied herself with the daughters of Charles VII as much as with her own children. Royal blood was valued so highly at this time that even bastards inherited something of that sacred quality which even illegitimacy could not impair.

§   §

The state of feeling at peace with himself, in which Agnes maintained Charles VII, the exaltation of love with which she inspired his hitherto suspicious heart, the chivalrous spirit which she created by her mere presence, strengthened the King for his task and added to his power and his pride. If he seemed about to yield to his former idleness and culpable indifference, she revived his energy whenever it failed and forced him to continue the work of restoration already begun. So the English began to lose ground and prestige, while the French, feeling a master near at hand, a leader ready to support them, gained a clear idea of the injustice of the foreign occupation and gradually shook off the heavy burden of supporting it. The struggle continued on both sides, but soon it became unequal under a king who had been aroused out of his morbid sloth. His faithful supporters kept a vigilant guard around him and continued their desperate struggle. Arthur, Earl of Richmond, appointed Constable of France, Dunois, La Hire, Xaintrailles, now restored to their old rank as military leaders, spared neither blood nor pains. The French troops especially showed their bravery. They took Chartres, then St. Denis and now they were before the walls of Paris.

Yielding to the diplomatic efforts of Yolande of Anjou and Agnes Sorel and wearied by the prolonged struggle which was bringing him no advantage, Philip of Burgundy finally consented to enter into negotiations with the King. The Treaty of Arras was the result. Three months were required to settle the terms. The English stood in its way. It needed the death of the Duke of Bedford, Regent of France, to make them decide to capitulate.

The English were forced to content themselves with Normandy and Aquitaine as sole pledges. The Duke of Burgundy gained the greatest advantage, for to him were ceded Macon, Auxerre, and the towns of the Somme; the complete independence of his states during his lifetime was granted as well. He also made the humiliating condition that the King on his knees should render him public atonement for the murder of his father at Montereau. Charles VII submitted, counting on the future to give him his revenge. A mass was said for the repose of the soul of the defunct duke, an abbey was founded on the spot where the crime had been committed, and all rancour appeared to be effaced.

At this moment, Queen Isabella, the King's mother, who had been living alone and deserted at her castle of Tournelles, died. The past seemed now to be dissolving with the passing of time and opposition began to melt away before the authority of the legitimate sovereign of France. The treaty was finally concluded on September 21, 1435. Now only Paris, in its turn, must yield.

There misery was at its height; artisans had no work and famine was raging. Throughout the whole land, but especially in the Ile-de-France, bands of raiders, called *les Ecorcheurs,* ravaged the country. They were made up of adventurers of all parties who had left the armies, disbanded soldiers who plundered in order to live, pillaged the country, cut down the vines and the grain, burned down the mills, violated the women and tortured the children. The environs of the capital were one vast desert. Epidemics laid waste the land and claimed thousands of victims.

"For this reason then," wrote Jean Jouvenel des Ursins in a letter addressed to the King, "I venture to say that you must awake and come to our aid, for we can bear no more."

The King was awakened, his lady by his side demanded feats of valour from her lover. To please her, he had become the Victorious; he would no longer fail in his tasks. His soldiers bearing the sacred fleur de lys were everywhere received as liberators. They captured Charenton, Vincennes, Corbeil, Brie, Comte Robert, St. Germain-en-Laye. To reassure the Parisians, who had done him grievous wrong, Charles promised to pardon all who had supported the English and the Burgundian revolt. The way was prepared for peace. The Constable, Richmond, entered the capital almost without a struggle. The English had taken refuge in the Bastille. On every side arose shouts of acclaim when the standard with the fleur de lys was waved high above their heads. Paris awaited, longed for the coming of her legitimate sovereign.

But he advanced slowly by short days' journeys, in small haste to return to the city of which, since his tragic childhood, he had preserved so unhappy a memory. At last, at the head of his troops, he arrived at Montereau on the first of October; he slept at St.

Denis, where the doors of the chapel were opened for him. Then he advanced to Pantin, to Bagnolet.

On November twelfth, finally, he arrived in Paris and made his solemn entrance into his capital.

§   §

It was a most affecting moment, the moment when Charles VII regained his capital, so long rebellious. For a hundred years past the enemy had disputed its possession and opposing parties had violated its memories. Heart of the kingdom, symbolic city, Paris, queen of France, the capital letter of French history, Paris now finds her King again, son of her kings. At every step memories arise to besiege the heart and fire the mind. A strange emotion must overwhelm any one who reads these last pages of this long secular struggle which removed the greatest danger ever facing a country. Paris now finds her King again, son of her kings. It hardly recognises his countenance and knows him only through the calumnies of his enemies, the English and the Burgundians, and through the mocking songs about his poverty and his weakness.

> My friends, what remains
> To this gentle Dauphin?
> Orléans and Beaugency,

Notre-Dame de Clèry
Vendôme . . .

That is what the bells of the cathedral of Orléans chimed, people said. But now that he is here, before their eyes, the Parisians tremble with emotion, for their memory begins to stir. He is Charles VII by name—that means that before him six kings named Charles have been sons of France, along with how many other kings named Louis and Philip and John! And this one had suffered much, had been driven out by his own brothers, had been obliged to reconquer what belonged to him by right. An affecting moment, this in which Paris now finds her King again, son of her kings! . . .

The Paris of Charles VII bore little resemblance, to be sure, to that of our days. The streets were narrow, the houses crowded close together in little clusters, but the various districts were separated by gardens, meadows, and vine arbours. The churches with their light steeples, as if carved by a sculptor, rose above the pointed roofs. Princely *hôtels* here and there proclaimed the dominant position of their lords. Three covered bridges crossed the Seine and the *Cité,* as to-day, was embraced in the two loving arms of the river. Notre-Dame, the Bastille, the Châtelet stood

forth in all their massive strength of stone. Farther
away, Ste. Geneviève, in the country, was only a place
for pilgrimages; in the *Pré-aux-Clercs,* or Scholars'
meadow, was situated the turbulent university. The
Hôtel des Tournelles, the residence of the kings, stood
surrounded by a forest of cherry trees and grape arbours. In the streets swarmed the people, active,
nervous as it has remained to this day, critical, witty.
Just as they had sung songs against the vanquished
King, so now they sang against the English.

> Well, well, we must rub up our leather
> Against the coming of the Duke of York.
> Return to your cold, northern winds
> And don't brag any more of fighting us.
> May the fever blast and waste you,
>
> .   .   .   .   .   .
>
> Best for you to depart on the spot
> And rid us of you for good and all!

The walls of the capital had been hung with white
and blue flags. From afar was heard the sound of gal-
loping horses, the King's horses, as he advanced from
St. Denis. The shouts of the populace preceded him.
Then the town council went forth to meet him, to welcome him and hand him the keys of the city.

Charles VII was clothed in the armour of war,

mounted on a splendid steed covered with a saddle-cloth of blue velvet sprinkled with fleur de lys. The Constable of France, Richmond, marched by his side, sword in hand, like the protecting guardian of his majesty. The Dauphin rode close by his father. Behind them came the Counts of Maine, Vendôme, Tancarville, and the Bastard of Orléans. The King dismounted before Notre-Dame and, after having made his prayers, advanced to the palace.

Along all the length of the march, bells rang and shouts of hurrah rose. At St. Lazare angels descended from heaven, bearing the shield of France upon their wings and singing with fresh, childish voices:

> Most excellent King and Lord,
> The people of your city
> Welcome you with all honour
> And in deep humility.

In the public squares the fountains flowed with hippocras instead of water and in their basins sported dolphins with silvery scales. On the platforms of the mountebanks in the streets the Passion of Arnoul Gréban was performed.

It was only fitting, surely, that Agnes should share in all this rejoicing, she who had been the secret, inciting influence that led to the fulfilment of the King's dream, the nameless accomplice in a policy of state-craft which made him conqueror as much as any tri-umph by arms. She must be present, proud, happy to behold her glorious lord, and she took part in the brilliant procession which accompanied the sovereign during his triumphal entry. She was watched with lively curiosity, for her liaison with the King was well-known. It was remarked that she was more beautiful than the Queen and the chroniclers describe her costume.

"She wore a bodice of red velvet adorned in front with the work of the goldsmiths' art, a mantle of ermine, a hennin embroidered with gold with a long azure veil floating like a wing down to the ground, shoes *à la poulaine*,[2] and ornaments of diamonds, with a necklace of gold and emeralds."

Supremely beautiful, Agnes passed through the midst of a dazzled people—dazzled, but muttering, too, for they were starving and had suffered too much during the last months of the war. She was known to them only through the rough jests of the Burgundians, the censure of the ignorant. If she was adored in Touraine, it was because there people saw how she lived and perceived her beneficent influence on the King.

[2] Shoes rising to a high point in front.

At Paris, a foreign city, long separated from the true,
loyal France of the banks of the Loire, the pamphlets
of the English circulated which repeated only one
thing: Agnes was the King's mistress, installed at
court, to the annoyance of the Queen who was greatly
disturbed by her presence. Though this showed complete ignorance of the actual facts, it was widely
credited. The *"Journal d'un Bourgeois de Paris,"* written at this time, expresses itself in the same vein and in
it one perceives how deeply rooted was the error on
the subject of one who was far from deserving the accusations with which she was overwhelmed:

"During the last week of April there came to Paris
a damsel who was publicly said to be the favourite of
the King of France, who was without faith, violating
the law, and without truth to the good queen whom
he had married, and it was very apparent that she lived
in as great state as a countess or duchess. And she came
and went, often with the good Queen of France, without having any shame for her sin because of which the
Queen had much grief in her heart; but she had to
endure this at the time. And the King, the more to
show and to make known his great sin and his great
shame, and that of her too, bestowed on her *the Chastel
de Beauté,* the most beautiful and attractive castle and

the most splendidly situated in all the Ile-de-France, and called her and caused her to be called the fair Agnes.

"And because the people of Paris did not render her as much reverence as her great pride demanded, which she could not conceal, she said at her departure that they were only low fellows, and that if she had heard beforehand that they would not do her more honour than they had done, she would never have entered the city nor set her foot in it, which would have been small pity. So departed the fair Agnes on the tenth day of May, continuing in her sin as before."

This good citizen of Paris who so well lives up to his name shows all the ignorance of the public which judges things from the outside without understanding the causes behind them. He takes Agnes for one of those light women who loiter on the streets of Paris and pities the Queen as if she were the wife of a merchant cheated of her conjugal prerogatives. Such lamentable judgment is the result of the petty moral standards of lower social classes which cannot distinguish between different stations in life and different situations and are incapable of separating the spirit from the letter, appearances from imperative realities. The church closed its eyes to this royal liaison and

never refused absolution to Charles VII at his annual
Easter sacraments. The Queen accepted the favourite,
loved her, and adopted her daughters, knowing her
husband as she did and recognising the good influence
exercised on him by this woman who guided him towards urgent measures of state.

Agnes, it is true, was wounded by this reception of
the people of Paris, ignorant of her true rôle in this
reconciliation between king and nation. Without her,
there is no doubt, it would not have taken place. She
never saw Paris again, preferring her native Touraine,
where her charity was known and her beneficent influence glorified.

CHAPTER III
The Fairest of the Fair

CHAPTER III

The Fairest of the Fair

THIS truce at last gave the country a breathing-space. An extraordinary cheerfulness began to spread over all France, depopulated, diminished and demoralised by the struggle of a hundred years. Its towns had been ruined, its roads destroyed, monuments and buildings in course of construction had been abandoned. To public calamities had been added cataclysms of nature before which human power stood helpless. In this year 1437, especially, the winter had been terrible. There had been one hundred and thirty-three days of frost so bitter that the Seine was frozen over and carts could be driven across it. Wolves had overrun the towns, devouring the living and unearthing the dead. Discouraged by their sufferings, men abandoned their labour, women their adornment.

But with the awakening of the King, the hour of the people's awakening sounded, too. The chronicler Chastelain writes that the French "are quick and energetic at their work, willing to take pains; they have active bodies, are not heavy, not sleepy, not idle nor slow, but always occupied whether with hands, minds, words, or deeds."

This impetus, this courage, this cheerfulness must be inspired from above. There is an old proverb of other days which says: "If the king yawns, the people grow tired." The people must have examples, stimulating suggestions, the right influences set before them. The King was not yawning now, he was smiling. He no longer slept, he acted, rejoicing in a happiness full of trust and confidence. To please his lady, he had become "the Victorious." Through her, he was about to become "the Well-Served." For herein lies the whole secret of successful rulers—to know how to gather around them those capable of assisting them in their difficult and unending tasks. All the great sovereigns have been well-served. Charles the Great, Louis VII, Charles V, Henry IV, Louis XIII, Louis XIV, and Napoleon were great because they knew how to recognise and choose from the nameless crowd of ambitious commoners and courtiers pressing around them those endowed with the intelligence and the loyalty to lend brilliance to their reigns. Ministers and advisers are the workers of the nations. Government cannot be carried on by one alone; there must be a head and the members of the body politic. France has not become what she is by her sovereigns alone, but by her servants under them. Suger, Richelieu, Colbert were all servants of the state. We may note that far from belonging to the nobility, these ministers, these advisers often sprang from the people of the *bourgeoisie*. They were often of the merchant class, citizens, or of the lesser nobility, like Richelieu.

So things came about, too, under Charles VII. When once the rough soldiers who understood nothing of statecraft were removed from his councils, when once Agnes Sorel had brought about a reconciliation between the prince and the great feudal lords, she surrounded him with men of intellectual power who completed the work of liberation begun by Jeanne d'Arc. The rôle of Agnes was to become the friend of those who had to be imposed upon the King; to be the channel through which flowed royal favour, and to aid in carrying out useful suggestions.

To restore the finances was the first care of the court. The time was not yet very far behind when the little "King of Bourges" had to pledge a diamond in order to live and had his boots mended because he could not afford to buy new ones; the time when Queen Marie requested the city of Tours, which wished to bestow a gift upon her, to give her useful

things which she lacked, such as linen, aprons, etc.
Money was needed and a man who would be clever in
providing it. In the Middle Ages only the Jews lent
money. Afterwards the Lombards monopolised the
banking business. Now it was a Frenchman who
offered his king the resources of his financial genius.
This Frenchman was a protégé of the house of Lor-
raine-Anjou. He became the friend of Agnes Sorel
who presented him at court, drew him into the immediate circle around the King, caused favours to be
granted to him, and through him created in the kingdom that new enterprise in business without which a
country is dead, like a corpse in which the blood no
longer circulates.

§   §

At Bourges, near the cathedral, there stands a house
which seems more like a palace, still in a state of perfect preservation. The approach is that of a fortress,
but the elegance of the façade, broken by mullioned
windows, corrects this impression. The sculptures
which one perceives as one approaches nearer are full
of imagination and seem to smile with a genuine welcome. It is the dwelling place of a strong man and an
artist.

THE PALACE OF JACQUES COEUR AT BOURGES

The balustrade which crowns the little terrace, above which rises the turret, is adorned with hearts and shells in alternate order, the arms of the master. So he combined his name with his destiny as a traveller—*Jacques Coeur.* This house, in its highly individual taste, is like an open book relating the story of the man who constructed it, one of the most interesting appearances in the political annals of France. Here are reversions to the Gothic and precursors of all the audacities of the Renaissance. The garland of flowers and fruits on the façade proclaim the epicure of life, an epicure who knows how to bite into life with all his might and to call all its vital forces to his aid. The details of the ornamentation, in the Oriental manner, tell of his voyages and proclaim how his very considerable fortune was gained. The interior court is at once an Italian court and a Moorish patio. His device which runs along it, intertwined with leaves, explains the success of this remarkable man! *"Faire, dire, taire,"* and *"À cœur vaillant, rien d'impossible."* [1] Who can resist the man who has the audacity to adventure and the still greater courage never to confide his ventures to others?

The father of Jacques Coeur, a native of Auvergne, was a merchant and furrier at Bourges under the happy

---

[1] "Act, speak, keep silent," and "Nothing is impossible to a valiant heart."

reign of Jean de Berry, the scholarly and artistic prince who possessed the finest library in the world at that time. This library passed on to Moulins under Anne de Beaujeu, then to Fontainebleau under Francis I, and later was to become one of the treasures of the French collection of the National Library. This furrier, Coeur, supplied furs to the court and to the great lords and so acquired one of the greatest fortunes of a man of his class at the time.

Jacques, his son, worked with him, married at an early age, in 1421, the daughter of the mayor of Bourges and was elected representative of Berry, and so became a member of one of the first families of the town. But he was not of a domestic temperament: he had vast curiosity, insatiable ambition, subtle understanding, and remarkable intelligence. To remain in his father's shop was not to his taste. Business attracted him, not, however, business that is done on the premises, but business transactions which extend out into the world. He knew the enormous profits to be realised in trading with Italy and the Levant. But was it really a fortune which he sought? No, his father had achieved that. Eager and ardent, artistic, imbued with the modern spirit, what he sought was adventure, the risk involved, the fever of gambling and danger. He had a horror of security, of immobility, of easy, monotonous happiness. With his associates, the brothers Godard, he founded one of those partnership-societies, called "companies" at that time, which had no cause to envy the gains of modern business companies. They arranged to supply the King and the great lords, almost gratuitously, with useful articles of merchandise, by way of publicity (again we see that there is nothing new under the sun), and to obtain in exchange certain privileges which would permit them to trade on easy terms.

Was Jacques Coeur guilty of manufacturing counterfeit money at this time, along with Bavant the Dane, as he was later accused of doing? Was he the director and farmer-general of several royal coinages? It is possible, but it is not certain. It has not been proved. In any event, it was at this time that he entered into relations with the House of Anjou which became very influential in business. Must we see, too, in Jacques' connection with Agnes the explanation of her sumptuous way of living, while her royal lover, still in want, could not provide her with the necessities? This remains a secret between the two. What is certain is that he becomes her friend, that she introduces him to the King, and that through her he receives the appointments of guardian of mines, master of currency, royal treasurer, guardian of the exchequer, charged with collecting the taxes and revenues of the domain. All this was, in fact, equivalent to having the title of minister of finance. Under the protection of the Queen of Sicily and as a zealous servant of the royal favourite, he procured for the King the enormous sums necessary for the reorganisation of the kingdom and the army. He established the gold standard and stabilised the currency. He had commercial relations with the whole Orient, to which he made numerous voyages. By his bold trading he advanced to Charles VII the money which enabled him to create anew his regular army and a serviceable fleet.

This was a prodigious adventure. They dreamed of it before Jacques Coeur's house at Bourges where the King and Agnes often came to visit him and where he offered them sumptuous repasts. They dreamed of it before the carved stone figures which, from false windows, look down upon and watch indiscreet passers-by or royal visitors. It is he, Jacques Coeur, who has made himself the richest man in the realm, who has the clear vision of a state which does not depend upon itself alone, exhausting and renewing its resources on the spot, but by bold exchanges and by well organised

JACQUES COEUR, SUPERINTENDENT OF FINANCES UNDER
CHARLES VII
Cabinet des Estampes
Bibliothèque Nationale

markets, connects the nation which it serves with the whole world which returns its treasures to it.

Jacques Coeur possesses seven galleasses, bearing the flag of the Holy Virgin: among them *Rose, Madeleine, Notre-Dame-St. Michel, Notre-Dame-St. Jacques, Notre-Dame-St. Denis.* He has light vessels for the coasting trade of Languedoc and Provence. He has barges with flat bottoms to unload merchandise which cannot otherwise be brought to port. He has a whole system of counting-houses, a sort of discount-banks for the immediate settlement of his contracts and his sales, in the ports of Marseilles, Honfleur, etc. He is remarkably modern and up-to-the-minute; he has foreseen everything, organised everything, observed everything.

The judgment which Georges Chastelain, the chronicler, expresses about him in these fitting words is not exaggerated: "He made the glory of his master resound in all lands and the jewels of his crown shine far over distant seas. He visited all the Levant in his ship and in the Eastern sea showed only the fleur de lys flying before his mast."

He displayed the growing glory of France in the leisurely voyages of his galleys. He brought to his country many products from foreign lands which filled it with even greater desires—sugar from Cyprus, cloves from Alexandria, green pepper, perfumed cinnamon. For the world of fashion he brought the gold cloths of Damascus, the velvets of Egypt, the satins of Cairo, the carpets of Persia and other countries of Asia.

He introduced the precious woods and the ivory of which the century to come was to make such artistic use. It was he who perfumed France with the incense of Tauris and of Bagdad, the musk of Tibet and of China, the amber of southern Arabia.

It was he who scattered rubies, sapphires and diamonds in profusion and bestowed on the real pearl its royal rank, always recognised since, for now pearl necklaces first began to adorn the throats of fair charmers. And it was he, the treasurer, the ship-owner, the regulator of currency, who supplied the queen of fashion, the all-powerful Favourite, who had gained him his favour, with everything that might add to her beauty.

Whenever a new cloth, a more brilliant colour, an especially finely cut jewel came into his hands, he offered it to Agnes, and the whole court, charmed by the novelty, would desire its like. So he anticipated Napoleon who had his wife Josephine wear the silks of Lyons in order to increase their popularity. Jacques

Cœur availed himself of the King's mistress as if she were a beautiful mannequin made to advertise his wares—so inventing the most modern form of publicity in addition to all the rest.

To these brilliant innovations must be added his achievement in re-establishing the fairs, abolished during the war like so much else. With all his other occupations, he combined his rôle as a diplomatist. It served his business, but his business served France. So, in 1447, he arranged an agreement with the Sultan of Egypt. He tried to annex Genoa to France; he intervened between the King and the pope. He is everywhere, he accomplishes everything, and when there is need to convince Charles VII of the urgency of a decision or a treaty, it is to Agnes that he confides the importance of the issue and its success, while he presents her with a new jewel. She is the channel of favours, she is the means of arranging and concluding agreements. So, at last, perceiving the strength of his position owing to his immense fortune and the vast services he rendered, she gained for him, in 1442, a dominant place in the grand council of state.

So much power is never acquired without risks. Through Agnes he has been able to realise his reformatory and life-giving mission. Like the King, he receives from her his consolation and his power. We shall see what befalls when his patroness will no longer be there to protect him, nor to defend Charles against himself. § §

This mission, which did not impede his personal success but which, rather, he was able to combine with it, was to restore life and vigour to the kingdom by causing gold to circulate and instilling a taste for luxury which the horrors of war had destroyed. The Favourite aided him not only by her costly expenditures for luxuries, but also for things that were useful. For example, she launched the fashion of wearing linen chemises. Before her time only wool was worn and the gowns were even worn next to the skin. Henceforth the daughters of kings received two linen chemises in their trousseaus and, in the spirit of imitation, the *bourgeoisie* followed suit, thus improving the national hygiene.

The treasurer, assisted by his friend, introduced the fashions of the Orient and of Venice, gold-figured brocades, shoes *à la poulaine* incrusted with precious stones, and the high head-dresses, resembling a bishop's mitre, which were called hennins.

Naturally all this did not escape criticism and this

criticism served to advertise the novelty. The preach-
ers soon grew busy and the hennin was denounced,
without any one's quite knowing why, as an occasion
for sin. It was enough that the King's mistress was the
first to wear one to render it suspect. A friar, Thomas
Couette, preached at all the crossroads to forbid women
to wear these extravagant head-dresses. When he did
not succeed in making himself heard, he stirred up the
children, starting them against the fashionable ladies,
with the cry, *"Au hennin, au hennin,"* as one cries,
"Au diable, au diable." The poor women fled, but the
next day they put on their head-dresses again. Since
those days the nuns have adopted these great wings of
white linen and so have assured them a long and
virtuous survival.

Agnes, the Fairest of the Fair, was fond of this arrangement which set off her wonderful face and her
beautiful form, of which she was very proud. We must
not, in explaining a character, make her insipid. Agnes
was a living being, a woman, her rôle was to create
life, to bring warmth into a circle which, before she
appeared, was frozen, immobile, paralysed by defeat
and terror. There was nothing mystic in her appearance. She was warm, she was sensuous. She was not a
courtesan, she was the King's mistress and, as sovereign

over him, turned him towards a life which must make him the ordaining leader of his kingdom.

From the criticisms of her contemporaries emerges a vivid impression of Agnes and another, also, from which she should be cleared:

"The king was much infatuated with this woman named Agnes, known and famed as such, and made innumerable great outlays contrary to honour, and caused himself to be greatly blamed for the position he bestowed on her because, in all Christendom, there was not a princess so splendidly arrayed as she nor one who could boast of such state."

". . . she wore trains a third longer than any princesses of the realm; higher head-dresses, more costly robes. And she displayed in her costumes everything that could lead to ribaldry and dissolute thoughts. She was always desirous of this and stopped at nothing, for she uncovered her shoulders and bosom as far down as to the middle of the breast."

"She had her own household in the King's palace, better ordered and appointed than that of the Queen. She was attended by a train with the sound of women around her and a greater number of them than the Queen, she enjoyed all the privileges of royal rank accorded her, as if she herself had been Queen, she had more beautiful bed-coverings, better tapestries, better linen and blankets," etc.

"Opposing all law and custom, whether of man or woman, devoting herself only to vanity, night and day, to mislead people and to create and give an example to modest women of the loss of honour, of shame, and of good morals, she was so skilful and practised in this respect that it was a pity for in the greater part of France and the adjoining borders, the whole sovereign sex was much contaminated in following her habits. She gained influence too over the nobility of the realm who, apparently given over wholly to vanity by her excess and her example, went astray and violated the obligations of their calling and the steady devotion to virtue."

In these unfriendly, censorious lines we hear again the Flemish chronicler, referred to before, who was under the influence of the Dauphin and he, as we shall see, was the enemy, or rather, became the enemy of the royal favourite out of hatred for his father. But the essential fact that stands out from these censorious comments is this: they show the influence that was exercised by Agnes not on morals—though hers were decent, aside from her liaison with the king—but on elegance, on fashion, on French luxury, revived by her. She thus lent aid to commerce and to industry, desperately injured by the long, calamitous war. She had been the cause of the King's awakening, now she aroused the kingdom. Her youthful vivacity influenced the whole court, stirring up opinion violently for or against her, which was a benefit in both cases. She enchanted her lover, whose spirit had been darkened by his tragic youth, she galvanised the court into life once more. Her policy in this respect was sound. It was later adopted by Francis I who insisted that his court ladies should appear in luxurious array to benefit commerce and increase his influence, which he wished to keep preponderant in Europe. Napoleon, too, followed this policy later, for he realised that the head of a state is not a monk and must not treat his realm like a convent that exists for the practise of privation.

The example set by Agnes and the court soon resulted in the resumption of business; gold began to flow into empty purses. The wives of the good citizens began to wear high bonnets with side-pieces of starched lawn, supported by threads of wire, which covered their caps in the form of Persian bonnets. The hair was drawn back or rolled, as Agnes wore it. When her coffin was opened in 1777, her magnificent head of chestnut-golden hair was still unchanged. It formed a veil over her forehead. At the back it was gathered in a heavy braid. Two locks fell down at the sides. But perhaps this was the arrangement for retiring, since her portraits show her, like her contemporaries, with face uncovered and hair drawn tight back.

Dresses now had become close-fitting, with tight bodices and sleeves, and exposed the bosom, with reveres turned back at the shoulders. The girdle, placed beneath the breasts, supported them, as if offering them as a lure to wantonness. The skirts were cut in such a way that they were drawn tight over the abdomen, while in the back they were full and extremely long. They were edged with fur, oftenest with ermine. The quality of a person was judged by the width of this fur trimming and the length of the train. Necklaces, girdles and rings were heavily carved in the Oriental fashion. Corsets were not yet invented and women wore wide bands of linen over the hips to confine the flesh firmly.

The magnificent dress of gallant warriors had always been extraordinary. In the book entitled *"Tournois du roi René"* we see how far the fantastic taste of captains and pages carried them. They not only wore rich Milanese armours of polished steel, but were arrayed in greatcoats of open-work cloth with multi-

coloured flaps called lambrequins. Jeanne d'Arc shared
in the folly of her century, so far as clothes were concerned. It was said that at her trial she had become
"ostentatious in her dress." The saint, like the Favourite, recognised the advantage that accrued from splendid array. To gain the obedience of her soldiers, she
must proclaim her superiority to the eye, a superiority
which represented her moral superiority.

The court of Charles VII, so long poverty-stricken
and meagre, under the influence of this reviving prosperity now organised its ceremonial and royal pomp
after the example of the courts of Burgundy and
Provence, the most luxurious of the age. Philip of Burgundy's ostentation was boundless. Vessels of gold and
of silver, tapestries and jewels blazed forth in halls
and on costumes. Dijon, the capital of the duchy, was a
splendid city, with its matchless palace. The Duke
loved brilliant festivities. At the marriage of Duke
John with Isabelle of Portugal, the merrymaking was
so great that the Flemings still preserve its memory in
wondering amazement. The citizens, great drinkers
of beer, were astonished to see before the palace, at one
side, a golden lion which for a full week never ceased
to pour out goblets of Rhenish wine; and at the other
side, a magnificent silver deer spilling forth streams of

the wines of Beaune, of Romanée, and of Malvoisie.

Here was exuberance of decoration and gesture, the cult of beauty! The cult of chivalry and honour, of which the founding of the Order of the Golden Fleece is the symbol! Courage carried to fantastic extremes, extravagant vows to achieve futile exploits expressed the spirit of the age. One knight swore never to rest in a soft bed until he had conquered twenty knights; another never to place hand on a woman's robe before he had broken twenty lances in single combat. In Burgundy reigned pomp and courage; in Provence poetry, art, imagination.

Good King René, husband of Isabelle of Lorraine and brother of Marie of Anjou, wife of Charles VII, had turned his city Aix into a capital of Beauty. An artist himself, a poet, a painter, a musician, he invented delightful plays which he has recorded in a beautifully illuminated volume called *"Les jeux du roi René."*

It was in honour of Charles VII and Agnes Sorel, who had come on a pilgrimage to Sainte Baume, situated in his flowery kingdom, that he conceived the most beautiful festivals. Provence in the month of May exhales a thousand enchanting odours. The rose, the carnation, the broomplant, the thyme perfume roads and gardens. René now planned a celebration which

lasted five days. There one saw King David, surrounded by devils and sorcerers, appearing in a procession of fairy-like splendour. There one saw Innocence protected by an angel in white; there one saw
the Golden Calf worshipped by the crowds ever devoted to the cult of riches. Dancers played on tabour-
pipe and timbrel and the people shouted their acclama-
tions to the King of France and the wonderful lady
who accompanied him in all her radiant youth and
beauty.

At Blois, another centre of art and beauty, Charles
of Orléans, returned from his English captivity and
married to Marie of Cleves, an exquisite woman of
literary tastes, assembled the poets of the age in tournaments of sentiment and verse. He himself recited his
rondeaux, ballades and triolets compounded of delight
and melancholy. The slow waves of the Loire bore to
Tours or to Chinon, which Charles and his Favourite
especially loved, the languorous echoes of this strange
music of sonorous words which still moves us to-day.

After the clash of arms and the clamour of the people, how sweet was this dream amidst the joy of living,
breathing, growing weary! The impulse towards
beauty and the example of refinement came from
princes. It is interesting to note that at this time the

great lords were also the great poets. There were
Charles of Orléans, Marie of Cleves, René, Philip the
Good. There were Margaret of Scotland, the Dauphiness; Jean de Bourbon, the Duke d'Alençon, the
Count d'Etampes, the Count de Nevers, the Count
de Vaudémont. They all wrote marvellous verse and
recorded their poems in beautiful books illuminated
by artists.

The universities, too, began to feel a new life. That
of Caën was created in 1432, along with those of
Poitiers and Bordeaux. François Villon was received
at Blois in spite of his poverty. Alain Chartier was the
guest of princes, Antoine de la Salle wrote his delightful novel about Petit Jehan de Saintre. A fever of
poetry and colour burned in men.

Flemish art prevailed above Italian art. The brothers
van Eyck were sought everywhere; the school of the
Loire began to flourish with its painters and sculptors.
There was Jehan Fouquet and soon after Michel
Colombe. The cathedrals which had been destroyed or
damaged were restored; those of Tours, Bourges,
Reims and Nevers were completed.

Music was now the folly of princes; they all had
their own chapels. Jan Van Ockeghem, the greatest
musician of the age, was captured by Charles VII who

entrusted to him the precentorship of St. Martin of Tours. Love, poetry, gallantry—these made up the century of Agnes, the fair, the charming, who filled the kingdom with the perfume of musk and amber offered to her by Jacques Coeur, lately returned from the Far East.

The long domination by a foreign foe, shaken off with a sudden fierce gesture by the exhausted nation, was concluded by a tournament. That of Tours is symbolic; it sums up the spirit of the time, it is the supreme form of expression of a deep hatred, a century old.

Jean de Bueil, Lord of Faye, of Montrésor, of St. Juliette and other places, Grand Master of the Archers of France, had been slain at Agincourt. His son Louis conceived a fierce hatred against the English. His insolence towards the last representatives of the invaders caused him to be challenged by a captain from across the channel, Jean de Chalons. An encounter between them was arranged to take place at Tours in 1446, the one to fight as champion of the king of France, the other of the king of England. A vast open space, west of the town, was selected; the court was present; the King, the Queen, and Agnes presided over the joust.

A platform, decorated with tapestries of red velvet embroidered in gold, surrounded the arena. At the centre of the galleries stood the chair of the King, who was to be the judge of the combat. An immense crowd had gathered and loudly acclaimed the sovereign when he appeared. Beneath the wintry sun shone forth the armour of the lords and the brocades of the ladies adorned in brilliant colours like those we see on packs of cards. Beside the Queen were her friend Agnes and the Dauphiness, Margaret of Scotland, lovely in her northern fairness. There were seen the Duke of Brittany, the Comtes d'Angoulême, Vendôme, Laval Tancarville and the Admiral Prégent de Coëtivy who had brought with him the second daughter of the King and of Agnes, little Marie of France. There were seen the Seneschal Pierre de Brézé, a friend of the favourite, to whom he owed his fortune. There were seen the episcopal robes of the Archbishop of Tours and of the Bishop of Vienne.

At the stroke of twelve, at noon, the barrier was opened. Jean de Chalons, champion of England, made his entrance. He was mounted on a charger caparisoned in black satin with a red cross in front and behind. He was escorted by the Sires de Dondelay, de Camus, and de Goote, an English lord. Before him marched squires bearing banners and lances, the trumpeters with the armourial bearings of the champion, which were gules with two fesses of silver and nine *mairl* of the same, placed four at the head, two in the middle, and three in the sharp end. Jean de Chalons presented himself before the King and the nobility, bowed to the assemblage, and rode around the lists. The pages, dressed in silver cloth, followed, leading two chargers. After the presentation, the procession withdrew to a corner of the arena.

At one o'clock a murmur again arose. Jean de Bueil, the French champion, now advanced. The trappings of his courser were covered with plates of silver enriched with precious stones, and magnificent white plumes waved above the croup of his saddle. He was preceded by two mules bearing caskets covered with vermilion velvet, with gilded bands, and by three steeds bearing his arms, which were sable, with three anilles of silver, placed two and one. These steeds were covered with little bells which tinkled at each step, in time with the trumpets. The six lances which preceded him were borne by knights of high degree who had fought in the war, Xaintrailles, Dunois, the brother of the Duke of Brittany, Charles of Anjou. The Duke of Sicily carried the helmet of the knight who was followed by pages on horseback, his head covered with white plumes.

Before entering the lists, Louis sent Pierre de Brézé to Charles VII to assure himself that his rival was of good family. On the assurance of the King, he made his obeisance and withdrew. Suddenly the trumpets sounded and the two champions dashed forward against each other with lightning speed. Chalons struck his adversary on the forearm, Bueil struck the Englishman in the neck. In the second onset neither landed a blow. In the third, the Frenchman's lance was splintered against the helmet of his foe. Again they rush forward. Bueil is wounded in the hand, his blood gushes forth. The combat is halted. But the adversaries, full of hatred, insist on continuing. Chalons then strikes his rival with such fury that his lance passes clean through his body. Carried back to his tent, Louis expired the same evening.

The next day his obsequies were solemnly celebrated in the cathedral at Tours. The funeral service was spoken by Adam Molyens, dean of the church of Salisbury, before the lords of France and the English ambassadors.

In this tournament there was more than merely a parade. This intentional ostentation of the two cham-

pions, showing them as rivals in elegance as well as in
courage; the two enemies, not on personal grounds but
in the cause of their countries, which were, nevertheless, now at peace, were symptomatic of an age of heroism, heroism that appeared superfluous, yet was necessary to maintain the moral plane of mankind. This
"post-war" feeling of the fifteenth century, which left
a sense of something incomplete and intolerable in
some hearts, is perhaps finer than the eager desire of
others to forget too quickly, in order to profit by the
gains for which the dead paid the price. Louis de Bueil,
the champion of France, was one of the pure flowers of
its chivalry and we like to remember that his son later
married Agnes Sorel's third daughter, Jeanne, in
whose veins ran the blood of the King who in this way
repaid his debt of honour to a family which had served
him well.

Beside this heroic knight, we may place a legendary
figure who shows another face of the declining nobility, enervated by long ages of over-breeding, that of
Gilles de Rais. It was at this same time that he became
the subject of common talk and his famous trial filled
the annals of the period by the side of the tournament
we have just described.

Gilles de Rais possessed immense domains between

the Loire and Poitu. Brave and intelligent, he, too, had been one of Jeanne d'Arc's companions in arms and she thought well of him. At twenty-five he was made marshal of France. The nervous excitation caused by abnormal habits, drunkenness, and lust consumed him and led him to commit a series of terrible crimes. He enticed young beggars, village children and women to follow him and had them taken to his castles of Tiffauges, Machecoul, and Chanptoce, where he subjected them to the worst tortures, violated them, cut their throats, or hanged them, feasting on their agonies in a curious mixture of sadism and sorcery. He was denounced after he had committed more than one hundred and forty crimes. After his arrest and trial, he was executed on the twentieth of October, 1440, in the meadow of Biesse near Nantes.

It was an age of moral and social confusion, the same causes leading to the same effects. At that time, as in ours, the war had caused wealth to change hands and power to change heads. The nobility had been exhausted by the long struggles and formed "the new poor" of that epoch. They were called the "mendicant-nobles." In order to exist, some of them requested to be enrolled among the citizenry, agreeing to forfeit their rank in order to live, for only citizens at that time had the right to engage in gainful work. The case of Guillaume de la Marche's wife may be cited who, after her husband's death, became a tavern-keeper. Some devoted themselves to agriculture, others to university studies, hitherto left to scholars. Still others entered certain trades which henceforth enjoyed the reputation of being noble trades, such as "masters of glass-making," "masters of iron-work." They laid aside their arrogance and entered into marriages with the wealthy citizenry.

Along with these new poor appeared the new rich, the citizens whom trade and business had greatly enriched, the butchers, the goldsmiths, the armourers especially. These now acquired immense wealth in land. Buying up the estates of the nobles, they became nobles in turn. Forewarned, they invested their wealth in the lucrative transactions opened up by Jacques Coeur; they took precedence of the old feudal nobility who had been ruined in the King's service and were now forced to yield to these newcomers the place which their deeds deserved.

History will always repeat itself in the course of the centuries; there will always be the perpetual swing of the pendulum from honour to money, a recurrence of new castes. One may ask what a bloody revolution has truly changed in this respect. The needs of the times bring about the exchange of social and material advantages peaceably. Evolution comes about by itself at certain critical epochs, without the need of violence.

The age of Agnes Sorel is the age of Louis de Bueil, knight of the white plume, of Gilles de Rais of scandalous morals, and of Jacques Coeur, genius in business.

Love, money, chivalry, the recurrence of new social classes—nothing is new and all remains the same.

But the Fairest of the Fair stands above the clashing forces with her divine smile which enchants the memory and which alone survives, a legend, because she is Beauty itself.

CHAPTER IV
The Dauphin, the Favourite, and the Rival

CHAPTER IV

The Dauphin, the Favourite, and the Rival

NATIONS, like individuals, have their rhythms, their curves, their rise and their fall of glory. An object of constant adulation, enriched, adored by the King, by queens, by the court, Agnes, queen of the kingdom's luxury and elegance, during her radiant youth dominated her age. But the moment came when her star slowly began to pale; without being eclipsed, it was transformed and she entered the realm of legend where her character and her accomplishment would be variously judged.

In her case the legend gathers nourishment from many sources. People are more interested in what is said about a person than about what he has actually done. The most splendid beings are only human and as such are subject to the wear and tear of time, subject to the law of change and subject to death. Life is terribly utilitarian. It makes use of every one's qualities and throws him aside when he is no longer needed. The happy accord of physical and moral resources with the circumstances they serve is ephemeral. When a person is no longer useful, he becomes troublesome;

the present rejects him, the future refuses him the tribute of admiration or appreciation which it owes him. We only occupy ourselves with certain romantic figures to stimulate our imagination, without studying their contribution of serious work made to history. This is life's ingratitude.

People speak of the ingratitude of the King towards Jeanne d'Arc. He behaved towards her only as we all behave towards others. Charles VII's ingratitude was certain, but unconscious. When the warrior Maid had once accomplished her mission, she had only to disappear; she was an embarrassing obstacle in the way of those who had made use of her. A little time was needed to strip her personality of a certain simple humanity, inconvenient to certain persons, and then to set her on a pedestal in history with all her prestige to be used again to advantage. For the King, for the church later, she became a torch. It had needed the funeral-pile at Rouen to make the flame burst forth.

Agnes Sorel played her rôle for her own day only. There is nothing more to be gained from her legend, and so it is assumed that it is not important that she is depreciated. Her usefulness died with her, while during her life all competed in serving her because all benefited by her. Placed beside the sullen King as a stimulus to his life and energy, the initial impulse given to him by her love, which he in turn communicated to his exhausted realm, might have continued thenceforth without her. She had been the inspirer, the instigator, by means of her youth and her beauty; the moment came when she could only be a woman like other women, taking up too much space to suit certain persons who had, none the less, profited by the favour which she had evoked in their behalf.

Just as the same circumstances, which lead to the same effects, always happen at the same crucial moment, in the years from 1440 to 1449 certain events occurred which warned the Favourite that the happy, splendid period of her life was over and that, like all others, she must undergo the assaults of sorrow and pain growing out of her too facile triumphs.

Doubtless she retained to the end her brilliant position; doubtless she still knew happy hours, doubtless the King remained wholly faithful to her. But she herself was waning; the future arose before her, eager to overtake her and ingulf her, and like wave riding upon wave, seemed about to throw her back into the abyss. She too had had a mission to fulfil. It was ended and she was left stranded. She must abandon a place which another was burning to seize.

We have seen that Agnes owed her good fortune to the Queen of Sicily, the King's mother-in-law. In 1442 Yolande of Anjou died at the château of Saumur. She was a figure of singular grandeur; strangely mysterious, little known, her rôle remains to be reported and glorified. It was she who, controlling the policies of the state and acting for the King, whose inadequacy she well understood, had supplied the means for his victories. True head of the House of Anjou, one of the most powerful feudal states of the realm, she was its last vigorous representative, uniting the greatness of its house to the House of France.

On the eighteenth of December, 1413, she had betrothed her daughter Marie to Charles, third son of Charles VI, then called Count of Ponthieu, who had no reason to expect to ascend the throne. At this time she took him away from his governors, Hughes de Noyers, Pierre de Beauvau, Hardouin de Maille; from his preceptor, Gérard Machet, who was later to become his confessor, and took him with her as if he were her son, a son disinherited by his own mother who was always a step-mother to him. He was never to part from Yolande again. She had him removed from Paris, then a prey to sedition, where his mother was leading a loose life, and brought him to Provence which he did not leave again until 1415. He was made Commander of Vincennes. Then his older brother, Louis, the Dauphin, died, and after him Jean, the second son, in the following year. Contrary to all expectation, Charles became heir to the throne. Yolande made of him her docile creature, her pampered darling, she loved and cherished him and of this he had great need.

"Repudiated because of fury and sedition towards the royal family, warred upon by his enemies, assailed by the swords and the words of his own subjects, half-heartedly obeyed by the rest of his people, deserted by his chief followers whom he should have been able to trust, deprived of his treasure, shut up in a fortress of contumacy"—so Alain Chartier in his "Quadrilogue invectif" described the King's position. The aid given to Charles by Yolande was miraculous. Without her the poor prince would have been lost, delivered over to his enemies; France would have been rent asunder without a legitimate heir to struggle against the English king. Charles knew this well, by the way, and vowed eternal gratitude to Yolande, who had been his providence.

"She whom we call our good mother," he said later in a letter, "in our early youth rendered us many great services and pleasures in various ways, which we must hold in everlasting memory."

As soon as Yolande left him, he became the prey of intriguers and favourites, incapable of defending himself. His nervous depression, due to his evil heredity and to the terrors to which he had been subjected as a child, made him feeble and helpless. He needed his mother-in-law near him to sustain and advise him. She married him to her daughter in 1422. As early as 1424, she arranged for a meeting between him and Arthur, Earl of Richmond, sovereign lord of Brittany, knowing how advantageous it would be to detach him from the English and win him over to their side. Under pressure from Yolande, Charles agreed to give all the necessary guaranties, however exorbitant, and to accept all the conditions made by the prince when he accepted the title of Constable of France.

M. Du Fresne de Beaucourt claimed to possess a document of which only eight lines remain, with the signatures of the King and of the Duke of Brittany, preliminary to an agreement witnessed at Saumur between Charles, the Queen of Sicily, and the Breton ambassadors, on the twenty-first of October, 1424. This document proves the preponderant part played by Yolande in all her son-in-law's undertakings and the intelligence with which she supported him.

The agreement with Richmond had as its corollary the alliance with Burgundy, which was to come later, and the reorganisation of the kingdom. These were the gains derived from the bargain with the new Constable. In return, the King handed over to him supreme control of affairs and left him free to exclude from the court those who displeased him. This was putting an end to the royal authority for the time being, and even to the personal liberty of Charles as a man. So Tanneguy du Chatel was sent away to Beaucaire with the title of seneschal to console him. Frottier d'Avaugour and Cadart, companions in their master's debauchery, disappeared. Louvet, president and administrator of finances, whose daughter had been the prince's mistress, resisted removal. Yolande took it upon herself to overrule him. In short, the King's entourage had first to be completely changed if there was to be a vigorous government. The King, incidentally, proved wonderfully docile. In the committee assembled to take all power from Louvet, he declared that he had been the victim of the president's importunities and had been ill advised.

"In the future he desired to act in accordance with

good counsel and to do all that his good brother of Brittany and his faithful Constable advised him to do."

This is the language of a child, not a king, and it meant submission to her who directed him. In her letter to the people of Lyons dated June 28th, 1425, Yolande clearly points out the rôle which she assigned to her collaborator, who was placed like a sword by the side of the prince: the Constable was "to take the necessary steps towards the relief of the kingdom and the union of the princes of the blood, to carry on justice and put an end to all plunder and pillage."

Charles was under the guardianship of his mother-in-law. At the meeting of the states-general at Orléans, he appeared accompanied by her and Richmond, who kept a trustworthy guard near him. Henceforth steps were taken for the restoration of the kingdom, henceforth the country was governed with a firm hand without suspecting who was the source of this firmness.

In the spirit of many other historians, Sismondi writes: "Up to this time Charles had appeared incapable of any attention or interest in his own affairs, incapable of acting energetically, of sacrificing his ease or his pleasures. From now on, to the contrary, we see him displaying a firm will to re-establish order in his kingdom, to drive out his enemies, to sacrifice his repose and his pleasures to his duty, and remarkable intelligence in his choice of means to arrive at his end."

This awakening, hailed as a miracle by all, was the result of Yolande's action. She was the energy, she was the good counsel, she was the one who truly saved the kingdom in distress. All whom she imposed upon Charles or conducted to him, whether it was Richmond or Jeanne d'Arc, became an artisan in the work of restoring France. With Agnes as her accomplice, she completed this work, putting into the mouth of the favourite the advice which she did not herself wish to give.

It was she again who gave to the King the stout sword which was to serve him in all his battles—Pierre de Brézé, squire of Anjou, who in 1437 was scarcely twenty-three years old and who had been in the service of Yolande and her sons. Knighted in 1434, he soon became Seneschal of Anjou and Commander of Angers. A brilliant, gallant knight, a fine talker, Chastelain said of him who played so great a rôle in this reign and in the next:

"He was the eagle of all the world; along with his wonderful valour, he was the best talker of his time and there were none, whether friend or foe, whom he could not convince by his speech, so much so that

whenever his sword could not prevail, his tongue conquered and mollified the powerful."

Through Agnes Sorel, who was his friend, he became a member of the council, with Jacques Coeur,
in 1441. Charles then bestowed upon him the château
and seigneuries of Nogent-le-Roi, Anet, Breval, and
Monchauvet.

This favour naturally displeased the courtiers who
murmured: "The Seneschal spoils all, destroys all, he
holds the King in subjection by the help of this Agnes
who is above the Queen."

In a secret report addressed in 1447 to the Duke of
Burgundy, we read: "The said Seneschal gets on mar-
vellously with the King, partly by the aid of Agnes
from whom he obtains what he wishes."

So the complicity of the Queen of Sicily, of the
Favourite, and of the new servitors of the king was
recognised. A net was woven around the feeble prince
by these two women and Yolande held the threads, to
the great profit of the kingdom, as all perceived.

That is why Yolande of Anjou is an important
figure, one whose influence has not yet been sufficiently
emphasised. This was partly her own fault, for she
neglected to force herself upon history. Supremely a
realist and supremely proud, she cared little for the

praise of men. The joy of acting, the success of her plans were enough to crown her. Her genius in statecraft, her finesse which even attained subtlety, reappeared in her grandson, Louis XI, and in her great-granddaughter, Anne de Beaujeu, who resembled her in many ways.

When Yolande passed away, Anges Sorel lost the benefit of her good counsel. Since this was no longer available, the King henceforth kept near him those advisers who assured the continuance of the effort that had been begun. Pierre de Brézé, the Seneschal; Richmond, the Constable; Bureau, Chief of Artillery; Jacques Coeur, Treasurer; Étienne Chevalier, the king's secretary and secret ambassador, were all her creatures, chosen from among all for their unquestionable ability.

With the death of Yolande, Agnes' political rôle was finished, a rôle, we may repeat, which consisted only of inducing the prince to accept the wise decisions of which she was not the author, but the instrument. She derived no personal satisfaction from it and Yolande's death affected her heart more than her ambition. She felt like an orphan, deprived of her great protection and her ever watchful affection.

§   §

But death cannot stop life. Life, especially at court, continued more intensely in proportion as prosperity was revived and increased. We have seen that after the Treaty of Arras a project for a marriage between the Princess of Anjou, René's daughter, and the King of England, had been worked out. Thanks to Brézé, the negotiations had finally been concluded. In April, 1444, at Montils-les-Tours, an extraordinary gathering of English ambassadors and French princes met for the final agreements. In April the Earl of Suffolk, Robert Ross, arrived at Blois; Dunois and Charles of Orléans accompanied them to Tours where they were presented to the Queen and to the Dauphiness. Jousts were organised, for in those days political agreements never took place without the accompaniment of popular sports. On the first of May a princely procession rode towards the meadows of the Loire, in honour of flowery May and the poet Charles of Orléans sang his wonderful songs with charming nonchalance.

> When I have heard the tabour sound
> Its call to welcome May . . .

The betrothal ceremonies between Margaret of Anjou and Henry VI of England took place in St. Martin's Church and the feast followed at the abbey of

MARGARET OF ANJOU, WIFE OF HENRY VI OF ENGLAND
Cabinet des Estampes
Bibliothèque Nationale

St. Julien. Scarcely were these over, when the rejoicing was followed by rare news. The King was at Nancy, on his return from the siege of Metz!

On the occasion of another marriage, that of Yolande, King René's second daughter, there were more festivities and dances. At that time the ladies of the court followed the armies very closely in order to celebrate their victories with them or console them in their defeats. The chroniclers describe tournaments and battles alternately, in the same language, for at this time courage was only another form of joy.

But King Charles himself was not fond of festivals. He suffered them without pleasure and preferred the intimacy of his châteaux on the Loire. "He was a recluse," people said. He spent the winter of 1445-46 at Montils or at Razilly, and there again his court arranged that famous tournament which has remained a model of all of that epoch.

§   §

But a great sorrow was lying in wait for him and Agnes, striking straight at their hearts, in the person of the little Scotch Dauphiness, with her disturbing charm and her brief destiny.

We have told of the arrival at Tours of this fair

princess from the north, married to the Dauphin in her eleventh year. No union could have been more unsuitable. The Dauphin, later to be Louis XI, was prosaic, exact, eager to rule. She was melancholy and tender, all poetry and languor. Delicate and fragile, her only passion was for books and poetry. Her messengers were charged to collect from everywhere beautiful manuscripts and learned treatises. She herself could compose and sing of her nostalgic longings for her native mists. Louis' feeling towards her very soon turned to aversion because her dowry remained unpaid and because she bore him no children. He hated her graceful tricks, her fragility, her charming femininity. Around her, as around the King's favourite who was her friend, deep hostilities soon arose. The taste they had in common for luxury, elegance, art, marked a new spirit which scandalised the survivors of the heroic days. Behind Agnes, coquettish and smiling, behind Margaret, enthusiastic and vibrant, stood jealous, angry duennas murmuring disapproval. The Dauphiness only laughed at all this, caring only for poetry and the love which inspired it. This passion was so strong in her that on her journeys she always carried with her coffers full of manuscripts. When the inspiration seized her, she abandoned herself to it with intoxication: "It was sunrise, before she retired, and once she was so interested in writing roundeaux, that she composed a dozen of them in one day."

Her soul was harmonious, her body was light. At the last festivals given by Charles VII at Chalons in June, she took part with Agnes in a ballet in seven parts. "She advanced taking four double steps, then three quick, short steps backward, then two, raised on her toes, four simple steps, and three leaps, finally two *congés.*"

One can see the aerial little princess in these lines, performing her dance. She had infinite allurement. Like the child she still was, she adored dainties, such as preserved pineapple and rose sugar. She was intellectual and alive. People called her complicated and perverse in her tastes, because she ate green apples and drank vinegar. She wore her dresses too tight around the waist and too full at the bottom. We read that she was affected in her toilettes, exaggerating the styles like our modern, spoiled young girls. But see her, lost in her books, when she is about to retire, while she comments mockingly: "My lord, the Dauphin, had had time to do a sum or two."

And for this he did not pardon her. They were opposed in their tastes and in their habits. She was extravagant and fond of show, he was saving and thrifty. She loved those who spoke beautifully, he detested useless words. To the official speechmakers of the various towns who advanced with a long roll of parchment in the hand, he used to say ruthlessly: "Be brief."

Yet he was jealous of the homage which surrounded his wife. It was through this jealousy that hostile bigots were able to take their revenge on her. It was commonly believed that Louis was seeking grounds to repudiate her. He had her spied upon cunningly by one of his cronies, Jamet du Tillay, who reported to the Dauphin all that she did, putting the worst interpretation upon it. Life between the pair became impossible. To escape from her unhappiness, Margaret devoted herself more and more to her books. Her nervousness increased. One day when she was at Chalons, she returned to the château, burning with fever. She undressed and, perhaps consciously wishing to put an end to her life, remained in the lower hall all night, reading and writing. She caught cold and became seriously ill. She could have recovered, but her only desire was to die. Indifferent to all attention rendered her, she remained pensive, as if far away from those surrounding her, her eyes already lost in infinity. They heard her murmur: "I swear by God and my soul and my baptism that I have not done my lord an ill turn or wrong."

When her death agony began, all around her wept except the Dauphin who remained calm and indifferent. She died on August 16th, 1446, at eleven o'clock at night, uttering these words, so sad in their expression of youth's disenchantment:

"Fi de la vie!" . . .[1]

Her obsequies took place in the cathedral of St. Étienne. Her husband was not present.

> She was a star, fair and light
> Sent to adorn this world.

So Martin Lefranc, the poet, sang of her; and her sister, Isabelle Stuart, Duchess of Brittany, put into her mouth these touching lines of which Margaret was the inspiration:

> Adieu, Dauphin, my dearest Lord—
> The lady begins to weep—
> For you I have crossed the seas . . .

> Adieu, noble Queen of France,
> And all our dear friends too.
> I shall beg our dear Lady
> To comfort my faithful spouse . . .

[1] "Fie on life!"

Adieu, Duchess of Burgundy,
My dear sister, Oh good, kind hearts,
If you can, in a thousand ways,
Bring peace to the fleur de lys . . .

Agnes and the King were deeply grieved. After their fostering mother, Yolande, this fair, tender flower of the court, the first Scotch Dauphiness, had passed away. The favourite now had no one on whom she could rely save the King who loved her with a constant, admiring love. He felt his source of strength in her. She had just presented him with a third daughter, born at Beauté-sur-Marne in 1445. On this occasion the King presented her with the château d'Issoudoun. Wealthy, provided with fine estates, all-powerful still, yet these dead forewarned her of the passing of all temporal things, of the frailty of all human joy.

"Fi de la vie!" Margaret had said, in breathing her last sigh. This despairing cry re-echoed in the heart of the young beauty, overwhelmed by grief.

"Fi de la vie!"

Robes and jewels, castles and lands, what were all these beside the treasures of the heart! And her heart was aching, wounded by the darts which struck it from many directions, sent by her enemies who wanted to strike her down by attacking at once her honour and her happiness.

"Fi de la vie!"

§   §

Out of the good that we think we are doing often is born an evil which we have not foreseen. Yolande of Anjou, to strengthen the tottering power of Charles VII, had rid him of his frivolous intimates and his rough captains, in order to cement the alliance between him and his great vassals. Though they had returned to the King of France, their legitimate suzerain, after having supported the English invader, these sovereign lords renounced none of their claims. The feudal chieftains, composed of the "lords of the fleur de lys" were becoming dangerous again. As powerful rulers who formed veritable provincial dynasties within the kingdom, they resisted the King and were ever ready to refuse him their support in order to guard their own prerogatives and their appanages. Soon after the Treaty of Arras, which they had helped to conclude, they again united and began to murmur against their ruler from whom they had not received the excessive benefits which they demanded. Accusing the royal favourite of being their adversary and of fostering the ambi-

tions of her own friends alone, they succeeded in en-
rolling in their leagues of malcontents the Dauphin,
impatient to assert himself.

Louis, the Dauphin, was born on July 3rd, 1423.
In spite of the hardships of that time, he had been
educated very carefully. He was kept at Loches with
his tutor, Jean Majoris, a pupil of Gerson, and his
governor, Bernard d'Armagnac, who both gave him
excellent instruction. He was highly intelligent,
shrewd and quick, was fond of study, and took intense
interest in the memorable events which were passing
before his eyes. He understood them, he passed judgment upon them, he would remember them for the
future. He saw Jeanne d'Arc, knew of her achievement, was present when his father regained his kingdom, accompanied him into his final battles and
entered Paris with him, already playing his part, burning with the desire to live, to direct, to act.

In 1436 the King established his son in his own
household. In 1439 he was entrusted with the defence
of Languedoc against the English. He was seventeen
years old, he was "treading on his father's heels," impatient to succeed him. He criticised his policy and
was especially displeased with his favourite whom he
accused of all the faults that he could find. She was

the friend of his wife, Margaret of Scotland, as we have said, and that was enough to make him hate her. Their engaging femininity, their affectations, their extravagant elegance threw him into a fury. He feared Agnes' influence and therefore fought it. Some have said that he hated her because she was preferred to his mother by the King. But we have seen with what good sense the Queen herself accepted this liaison. Far from suffering under it, she knew that it was necessary.

A document of the school of Chartres tells us that in 1444 the Dauphin offered the Lady of Beauty a number of magnificent tapestries. What was the motive behind this generosity? Some have held that Louis was in love with Agnes, but this interpretation is scarcely in accord with his nature. We must rather see in this gesture an attempt to win her over. He wanted to try to assure himself of her support and to cease attacking her in the dark. But Agnes saw through him; she paid no attention to his self-interested advances.

Henceforth, not being able to win her over, he was determined to get rid of her, in order that he might dominate more strongly the feeble spirit of Charles VII, now supported and instructed by her watchful friends. Louis became the author of all the calumnies

which were whispered about the favourite. He even
attempted to lead her into temptation, so that, by a
sentimental betrayal, she might be detached from the
King. So he hatched a little plot with his friend Chabannes on which he built great hopes.

The Count of Chabannes, a good talker and a gallant gentleman, at the Dauphin's instigation feigned
a great passion for the Fairest of the Fair. He pursued
her for some time with assiduous attentions and one
day, to hasten the climax, he threw himself at her feet
and declared his passion. The favourite, greatly
startled, arose and reported the matter to the King,
who banished Chabannes from court. Louis could
scarcely restrain his rage. One day when by chance
he was with her at Chinon in the great hall, he
broke into violent abuse. Charles replied sharply. Unable to control himself, Louis cried: "By our Lord's
passion, this woman is the cause of all our misfortunes," and struck her in the face.

The King drove him from his presence. Then he
allied himself with the Duke of Bourbon, d'Alençon,
and others. Together they formed what was called the
Praguerie, in allusion to the recent insurrections of the
Hussites in Bohemia, with Prague as the centre. Louis
even conceived the plan of carrying off his father to

the Château of Razilly. He would have claimed the office of regent on the ground that Charles was incapable of ruling, like his father, Charles VI. He disclosed this project to Chabannes who, seeing here an opportunity to restore himself to the royal good graces, revealed the plot. A special committee met at Candes and several Scotch guards, who had been accomplices in the plot, were executed. Charles VII took up arms against the rebels, struck at them at Poitou, at Auvergne, at Bourbonnais. They hastened to implore pardon. Louis was exiled to Dauphiné.

Pope Pius II wrote at this time: "Agnes was the cause of many disorders and of the Dauphin's flight." Rather we may say that she supported the father against his ambitious son, and many never forgave her for this.

Once in Dauphiné, Louis installed himself as a sovereign, practising his hand at ruling, instituting reforms which later were to establish his glory, for this bad son was a great king. There he remained, constantly spinning intrigues against the court, up to the day when the King sent an emissary to seize him. He was with his mistress, the lady of Sassenage, at the time, when he was warned that the King's men-at-arms were seeking him. He jumped out of the window and fled, without stopping, to the Duke of Burgundy.

When he learned of this flight, Charles VII cried: "My cousin of Burgundy is keeping a fox who will eat his hens."

But Louis was not yet content to remain inactive. From his exile he wrote his father one of those wheedling letters of which he was master: "My sovereign lord," he said, "I commend myself very humbly to your good graces. I beg you to send me your good wishes to achieve them."

He set conditions for his return. The first was that Agnes Sorel must go. Charles replied to his son in the same vein of cunning, assumed good feeling but he did not recall him nor did he separate from her whom he loved. Father and son never saw each other again.

Not being able to attain his ends through the woman, Louis began to attack the friends of Charles, the men with whom Yolande had surrounded him in order to complete the work of national reconstruction. The ingenuity of the prince is almost incredible; all means were good that helped him to arrive at his goal. "The King," said he to his companions, "manages his affairs as badly as possible. I intend to put things in order. When I return, I shall drive away Agnes and shall put an end to all his follies, and things will go much better than they are now."

He succeeded in one thing at least—for a moment he shook Brézé's position. The Seneschal had employed an agent of the Dauphin named Mariette, as a counter-spy, as we should say to-day. Mariette played a double game, receiving payment from both and belonging to the side that paid him best at the moment. Betraying both masters, he got them in turn into critical positions. The result was that the King's suspicions were aroused against his Seneschal. It was, however, only a passing shadow, and Louis was not satisfied with this. It was not long before a new storm was breaking.

Brézé was engaged during the winter of 1447-48 in the capture of Le Mans, still held by the English at that time. On his return, a formal denunciation was brought against him by the Dauphin, who offered to prove his charges. Some time before October, 1447, one of the King's secretaries had been arraigned before a royal court of justice, accused of having entered supercharges in letters of the King providing for certain administrative commissions and of having misused blank signatures. The accused was no other than Mariette. He had been imprisoned first at Loches and later transferred to Lyons. He succeeded in escaping from there and made straight for Dauphiné, where he fancied he would find a refuge with his young master. But Louis had him arrested and put to the torture, so that, through Mariette's accusations, he might ruin Brézé, even at the risk of revelations which might compromise himself. And so it befell, for Mariette told of the various missions he had accepted from both Louis and Brézé. He was transferred to Tours and then to Paris, there condemned to death by a decree of the court, and quartered and beheaded.

Of what, exactly, was Brézé accused? The records have been lost. Whatever it was, he saw that he must confront his enemy and demanded that the King let him be judged, holding himself as prisoner pending the verdict.

"In spite of the grave and criminal charges of which he was the object," the report of the trial declares, "Brézé exculpated and exonerated himself at great length, in such a way and with such convincing reasons that the king was satisfied."

But it is also reported that during the trial of the Seneschal, the Lady of Beauty arrived at Paris with a magnificent train, to make a pilgrimage to Ste. Geneviève, as she said. She was accompanied by Guillaume

Gouffier and Poncet de la Rivière. The Favourite came in person to plead the cause of her "very dear friend and companion."

With such a pleader, the prisoner's cause became very hopeful. Brézé obtained his formal pardon the next winter. In this document mention is made of the services he had rendered and of others that were expected of him. His offices and his property were restored to him.

Again Louis had failed in his perfidious attacks against the woman he hated.

§   §

The heart of Agnes was suffering its first sorrows. The death of her two women friends, Yolande and Margaret; the persistent hatred of the Dauphin, which had repercussions at court, where he always had spies watching her; the division between father and son, of which she was not the cause but the pretext, struck her hard, now that her youth was waning. The King, however, preserved his love and favour towards her undivided. "Hands off the favourite!" was the rule and if one wished to turn Charles against a courtier, all that was necessary was to say that the courtier had spoken ill of Agnes. He still preserved the memory of the wonder and delight of their first meetings.

There is a story, perhaps only a legend, recorded in the memoirs of the period. Though it may be apocryphal, it shows how the undying attachment of the King to his beloved mistress was regarded.

Whenever the interests of the kingdom demanded it, the favourite understood how to efface herself and sent Charles VII where his duty called him. If he desired her presence during an unusually long campaign, she joined him and brought to his tent the enchantment, ever renewed, of her white arms and her soft throat. One evening, at the château de Bois-Trousseau, a gift of the King on the birth of their daughter, she was dreaming of the absent one and thinking of her recent sorrows, so little in accord with her smiling face; of the hatred against her, so little suited to her gentleness, when her servants reported that a knight, exhausted and weary, requested her hospitality. Agnes ordered that he be given asylum and entertainment until the morrow. The knight was brought before her and knelt before the lady courteously, to thank her for her kindness. When he arose, she recognised her lord and fell into his arms.

Charles, overwhelmed by his desire to see her, had left behind his affairs of state and approached his beloved in the guise of a timid young lad. As it seemed best to keep these rendezvous secret, since the times were uncertain and the roads dangerous, it was arranged that whenever Agnes could receive her lover, she should light, at the top of the tower, a brilliant torch for which signal Charles would watch at night. Then, leaving everything behind, he would hasten to her who had made him forget the cares of his reign and the fears his nature was prone to, to her who, along with tenderness and delight, now gave him the strength to hold out, as she had first given him the strength to rise. Those who deny this influence surely forget or do not understand what a woman can do in the life of a man overwhelmed by responsibility and succumbing beneath the burden of a destiny too great for him.

This legend or this story is still kept alive at le Berry. The traveller is always shown, at the summit of a wooded hill, the remains of a ruined tower which is still called "the signal tower."

§   §

It was, of course, quite impossible that the King's constancy and Agnes' good fortune in the face of her political adversaries should not arouse the envy of men and above all the envy of women. If the great feudal lords, with the Dauphin at their head, sought to diminish her power because they wanted the share which she bestowed on her friends in the government, women, too, strove to harm her since they wished to capture for their own advantage the magnificence of the invincible favourite. More than one dreamed of supplanting her, one above all struggled to attain this and in the end succeeded her.

We have said that Agnes had been reared in Picardy with a younger cousin, Antoinette de Maignelais. Distinguished by great beauty like Agnes, she lacked the charm of the Lady of Beauty, that charm which had made her fortune, that sweetness, that softness which made her presence as soothing and enchanting as a lovely flower. A secret jealousy had always been hidden in Antoinette's heart; the Favourite did not suspect it or at least she did not realise its full danger. She feared her cousin so little that, at the height of her favour, she felt a desire to see the companion of her early years again. She sent Étienne Chevalier, her faithful friend, to Picardy to fetch her cousin to see her. Charles VII's secretary started forth and this is the letter he wrote to the Lady of Beauty, in giving her the account of his journey:

"I have experienced very great difficulties, Madame,

during the whole course of this journey, but in the last few days such difficulties have presented themselves that truly if our divine Saviour had not aided me with his all-powerful protection, I should probably have perished, body and soul. The accursed English, enemies of our lord the King and of the fair land of France, overran all the country along the Oise, but they have been conquered, and with them the obstacles which I encountered in Picardy.

"I finally reached the walls of the castle on foot . . . following your instructions, I requested to speak to your aunt, but, alas, the poor lady has departed from this life to another.

"Greatly surprised, too, not to see old Enguerrand appearing before me, as you had informed me, I eagerly asked where he was. I was informed that he too was no longer living and that the only person now at the château was Mademoiselle de Maignelais, your cousin. On requesting that I be conducted to her, I was taken into an enormous hall. When I had conveyed to the young lady the mission with which you had honoured me, she reflected for a moment and then replied coldly: 'I shall go, sir.'

"She gave orders, nevertheless, that Monsieur, your ambassador, should be well looked after.

"When I asked her if she planned to start soon, informing her that the roads were very unsafe and that, if she would allow it, I would accompany her as far as Chinon, she assured me that her preparations would be completed in a few days and that after she had given some indispensable orders to her people, she would not delay her departure an instant.

"Happy in this assurance, I send you this letter, Madame, so that you may be ready to receive Mademoiselle de Maignelais. I can, moreover, assure you that whatever were the perils which I had to brave to fulfil my mission, I am quite ready to begin it again and to go even farther, if such is your good pleasure."

This letter reached Chinon almost at the same time as the writer, since the post was anything but fast in those difficult times. Étienne Chevalier acted as Antoinette's escort and brought her to Agnes. One can imagine what the feelings of the two cousins must have been on finding themselves face to face again, after so many years. Agnes, when she lived with her aunt, had been an orphan. She had been an orphan who was cherished, adored and even preferred, as we have said, to Madame de Maignelais' own daughter, but none the less, she had only her sweetness and her beauty by which to gain and hold the favour and the attention of which she was the object. But now this favour had carried her to the pinnacle of power and honours, she was more than queen, she was the mother of the King's daughters, she possessed not only one château but several, her wealth could not be estimated, and her elegance, maintained by the treasurer, Jacques Coeur, was famous through all Christian lands. She outshone Queen Marie, who always looked a bit mean because of her avaricious nature.

Now Antoinette, in turn, had become "the orphan." Of the lesser nobility and relegated to her province, she was no longer dominant, but subordinate. All the graciousness of Agnes' welcome could not lessen the shock which her slumbering jealousy dealt to her pride. She measured the distance that separated her from the King's favourite, she realised that it was immeasurable and, without daring to hope to supplant her in the King's mind, she undoubtedly felt a terrible desire to do so.

Some believe that Antoinette bore a grudge against her cousin because of her equivocal position at court. She might have confided to her the chagrin of her dying mother on learning the rôle of her niece beside Charles. But we must not credit this in the least. In that age of liberal morality, the title of favourite (and

Agnes was the first in history who bore this name), the rôle was esteemed glorious and enviable. The favourite is the first wheel in the great political machine. On her intelligence, her adroitness, her integrity depend the happiness of the King and the happiness of the people. Sovereign mistress because of her physical attraction, she may be useful or harmful to those about her. She must therefore be flattered and respected rather than decried.

Antoinette, for whom fate held in reserve a deplorable rôle, could not possibly express a censure which she was far from feeling. She envied Agnes her place without belittling it in any way in her heart. She envied it so deeply that at this moment was born in her mind the desire to supplant her cousin. Charles, to be sure, loved his mistress and the daughters whom she had given him. But does not habit in the end always succeed in taking the edge off pleasure and the most ardent feelings of devotion in the heart of sensual men like Charles? Was he not dissolute and easily tempted before the coming of the damsel of Fromenteau? Perhaps the beast still slumbered in him, unsatiated, which had delivered him over in his youth to all sorts of vices and all sorts of pleasures? Agnes with her fair beauty had captured him, enchanted him, made him wise.

She had made him King, and a Victorious King, but would the hour not strike when his old habits would awaken, now that Yolande of Anjou was no longer there to watch over her son-in-law and support the charmer whom she had placed by his side to restrain his evil instincts?

Antoinette too was beautiful. Beautiful and wicked. Wicked and designing, ready for any betrayal.

And then it was, exactly, that the King came to Chinon to visit his mistress. He saw the cousin and undoubtedly paid very little attention to her at this time. But the cunning young woman probably watched him carefully to study his weaknesses. She was clever enough too to gain his interest in her behalf in the matter of having some lands of Maignelais restored to her, which the Duke of Bourbon, with whom she was engaged in a lawsuit, was withholding. When she had obtained this favour, she came to the conclusion that her hour had not yet struck and returned to her château, promising herself to return.

But Agnes was too shrewd not to know that the glance of a jealous woman had rested upon her, that a shadow had fallen between her and Charles, a shadow as light as that of a cloud, a shadow of the vaguest but also the saddest presentiments.

CHAPTER V
Death, Sole Victor over Love

CHAPTER V

Death, Sole Victor over Love

THE hour comes to us all when all that has lent value to life seems to shrink and grow less significant. The relative importance of all things becomes cruelly clear. We must return to fundamental principles, to firm supports on which we can lean to avoid a feeling of dizziness, the whirling dizziness inherent in all consciousness which has experienced the round of pleasures and advantages which we believed real and which we find in the end to be vanity. Youth carries with it a sort of intoxication and all that one sees in its radiance seems marvellous. The passing days dim its brilliance and the most fortunate men as well as the poorest, the most beautiful women as well as the most forlorn, share in a common destiny. Then, only the gifts of the heart appear valuable, lasting, immortal, beyond temptations and appearances.

Agnes, now admonished by the warning strokes of Fate, would not have been rated rich in fortune if she had been merely a beauty. She would not have deserved attention if she had been splendid because of her fortune alone. Her glory was perishable since it was supported by royal favour alone. If posterity still owes her homage it is not only because she was the instrument of a stronger will which, as we have seen, made use of all the resources offered to attain its ends. Her political rôle ended with the death of Yolande. She became useless when once the kingdom awoke from its torpor under the stimulus of the energetic action of its chief. There is Jeanne d'Arc's mission to remember. There is also her soul. Just so, there is Agnes Sorel's mission and there is also her soul; and her soul deserves to be loved and praised. Under any conditions she would have been remarkable, in any situations she would have been remarked. Her life was only a flowing out of her tenderness, her generosity, her sweetness. All who approached her bore witness to her kindness, her sympathy. She felt that she was not really the possessor, but merely the guardian of the gifts of which she was the occasion, not the end.

Monstrelet has said truly: "So this Agnes was of a very charitable way of life and liberal in alms-giving, and of her possessions she distributed widely to the poor, to the churches and to beggars."

There remain only five letters of Agnes, written by her with her autograph and held to be authentic, and

ENGUERRAND DE MONSTRELET, THE CHRONICLER
Who First Wrote of Jeanne d'Arc and Agnes Sorel
Recueil d'Arras

all these letters record acts of kindness. The first is addressed to La Chesnaye, in behalf of some poor men accused of having taken wood from the forest, who were about to be punished severely.

MONSIEUR LE PRÉVOT,

I have heard that several men of the parish of La Chesnaye have been summoned before you on suspicion of having taken wood from the forest of that place and that a day has been set to hold an inquiry regarding their innocence.

Having learned in this matter that all of these men mentioned are poor, wretched creatures, and that they suffer great misery in providing for the lives and subsistence of themselves, their wives and their children, I do not wish that any action be taken against them beyond this inquiry and summons, nor that the said persons be deprived of their freedom or of their goods, but on the contrary that the said action against them be rendered null and void and in carrying this out without delay you will render me a kind service. etc.

Your good mistress,

AGNES.

At that time, as to-day, a financier could steal millions and remain respectable, but a poor man for taking a few sticks would be handed over to justice. Agnes made amends for justice by her charity.

In another letter she shows pity for animals, those other victims of human wickedness.

To Mademoiselle de Belleville,

Mademoiselle, dear friend, I send hearty greetings to you. May it please you to know that I am surprised to hear the report which you sent to me by young Dampierre and I return it to you to aid you in overcoming what must have caused you great vexation.

May it please you to know that we are enjoying ourselves as much as possible in this neighbourhood and you ought to come here as soon as you have done with this annoyance, which I hope will be soon. Meanwhile we yesterday hunted a wild boar the trail of which was found by your little dog Robin, but the hunt turned out ill, to the detriment of your little Robin, as he was struck by a dart which one of the hunters thought he was sending against the boar in the thicket, and he received a rather serious wound.

But we hope that it will heal very soon and he shall be very carefully guarded. In the meantime, if there is anything else which I can do for you while awaiting your return, let me know and I shall do it with great pleasure, etc.

AGNES.

He who loves animals has a compassionate heart. She writes a second time to this Demoiselle de Belleville in regard to another dog which she entrusts to her friend with that persuasive sweetness which was one of her charms.

Will it please you, too, to receive my greyhound Carpet which I beg you to keep near you; and not allow him to fol-

low the hunt with any one, because he obeys neither whistle
nor call; which is the reason why I send him back, as otherwise he would be as good as lost. So you have him entrusted
to you, my dear friend, and may you do me this pleasure,
praying God to give you his grace.

At Razilly this VIIIᵉ day of September

Your very good friend

AGNES.

Next comes a letter addressed to Pierre de Brézé,
Seigneur de la Varenne, who was, as we have seen, a
protégé of Yolande and a friend of the favourite, to the
great disgust of the Dauphin.

To my very honoured Lord and friend, Monsieur de la
Varenne, Chamberlain to the King,

Monsieur my friend, I send greetings and commend myself to you and especially I request your favour in behalf
of one named Mathelin Tiéry who is the father of some of
my servants here who has let me know that an income which
he counted on receiving from his butcher's shop in the city
of Chinon to the amount of 22 sous has been so much reduced as a result of the wars that at present it is worth only
16 sous; which added to the little that remains to him does
not permit him to live and so he has fallen into dire poverty;
so as a suppliant in behalf of said Mathelin I beg that you
will graciously agree to condescend to give him some em-
ployment, which was promised him by your squire Guionet,
the which will come most opportunely for his maintenance.

This, then, is what I would request you to grant and to

yield to him graciously, the which will come as an indemnity to the said Mathelin for having been severely used in the matter of said income, and you will be doing me a great favour in hastening this matter.

At Cussay, the penultimate day of April.

Your servant and friend,

AGNES.

Cussay is in Touraine, like Chinon, Razilly, and Amboise, from where the following letter is dated. Agnes' personality is wholly in harmony with the soft, variegated sky of Touraine beneath which she passed her life. Their languors are similar; the charm of Agnes is comparable to the charm of Touraine. Against the horizon of the Loire we see revealed the soft, gracious curves of her silhouette—the lady called the Fairest of the Fair, all white and rose-coloured, followed by Carpet, her greyhound, which "obeys neither whistle nor call," long and slender like her train and white like her hennin.

It was there too that the King was happiest in the intimacy of his favourite château, where he played chess and gave ear to his musicians. It was there that he found his first kingdom and there he had his capital. The following letter gives proof of the King's love for the province of Touraine, the royal province from which he never parted without regret.

To Monsieur de la Varenne,

Monsieur my dear friend and good comrade, I refer to you as earnestly as I can the following: I am sending to you the letters of reprieve regarding the homage of la Fresnaye, begging you conjointly to take up this matter and asking you to do me the service to carry it through, not being able to decide to leave; and in this request he [the King] attests that he has no mind to forego remaining there.

.   .   .   .

Written at Amboise this eighteenth day of August.
Your very good friend and comrade,
AGNES.

So, whether it is for little dogs, or for the father of her servants, or for poor people in trouble, Agnes' heart is full of pity and overflowing with kindness. But was this heart completely and always devoted to Charles, the King who must always be guarded against himself and protected from the assaults of melancholy and his own instincts? He was generous, he was good, undoubtedly; but how ugly he was with his loose mouth, his round eyes, his bald skull, his weak, knock-kneed legs, this King as Fouquet shows him in the painting at the Louvre. . . . None the less, it is certain that the young woman was absolutely faithful to him. Gentle and smiling, she tried to please only him. She was so spied upon, watched with such suspicion and jealousy, that the least suggestion of any wrong would have been exploited as proof against her reputation. Yet no name is ever associated with hers as a lover.

No name? Yes, there is one, whose rôle must be explained: Étienne Chevalier, Seigneur de Vigneau, du Plessis-le-comte, councillor and private secretary to the kings Charles VII and Louis XI, ambassador to England and to Italy. He was born in 1410 and was of the same age as Agnes. Charles had knighted him himself, saying to him: "You shall be chevalier in fact as in name."

He was a very singular personage, a scholar, a minister, and a patron of the arts, possessing the most beautiful books and the richest bindings with marvellous illuminations. A lover of beauty in all its forms, his portrait shows us a strange visage, serious and pale. His hair formed a crown above his head, his nose was long and knowing, his eye melancholy and intelligent, his chin sharp. His face showed a bony structure as if carved in old ivory. He lived on very intimate footing with the court, as a secret minister whose rôle has not been definitely determined but which was certainly important. The King overwhelmed him with favours and honours, undoubtedly as a high reward for his services.

ÉTIENNE CHEVALIER AND ST. ÉTIENNE
From the Panel by Jehan Fouquet in the Museum of Berlin

The fact that Louis XI later retained him by his side is sufficient proof that this cunning prince must have recognised his ability.

Étienne Chevalier, as a friend of the arts, was Jehan Fouquet's patron. It was he who ordered the artist to paint the famous diptych, the two panels of which are separated to-day, the one being at Antwerp, the other at Berlin. They present a disturbing enigma. The right panel represents the Virgin Mary; the left, the donor, kneeling and contemplating the mother of God, praying to her in ecstasy. This donor is Étienne Chevalier himself, with his knowing face, with an expression like Voltaire's. His patron saint, St. Étienne, is presenting him to the Virgin Mary, as was the custom. He seems to be barely forty years old, which places the painting near 1549.

The Virgin Mary is no other than Agnes. She has Agnes' countenance with the pure features, the nose delicately tilted, the mouth as dainty and red as a fruit, the fine line of the eyebrows which were shaved in that day as in ours to perfect the curve of the arch. She is wearing an ermine mantle, symbol of her secret royalty; her corselet reveals her bosom, a marvel of the beauty of the flesh, pure yet disturbing. Is this really a Virgin portrayed here? Is it to this slightly daring

representation, or to this perfect bosom revealed to his
eyes, that the donor is offering his profane prayer,
dedicating his ecstasy and his adoration? No one will
ever know, because no one learned his secret. We may
be sure that he did not betray his King who had abso-
lute confidence in him. When Charles had to be absent, it was to Chevalier that he entrusted what was
dearest in the world to him. No one ever surprised
them in culpable intimacy. Yet there was complete
confidence between them and later it was he, along
with Jacques Coeur, whom Agnes appointed as the
executor of her last will and testament. As for him,
he seemed obsessed by the Lady of Beauty. On his
shield was inscribed this rebus, easily interpreted:
"Tant elle vaut celle pour qui je meurs." [1]

At his mansion in Paris, Étienne had carved in
the midst of a golden frond this other mysterious
distich: *"Rien sur L n'a regard."* ("Sur L," that is
Sorel.) [2]

This may have been a secret romance, perhaps a
mysterious, pure devotion. Chevalier undoubtedly
loved Agnes with deep, respectful love, and in conse-

---

[1] "She for whom I would die is well worth as much as this." A pun is implied
for the word for shield, *ecu*, also meant *crown*.

[2] "Nothing equals Sur L."

AGNES SOREL AS THE MADONNA
From the Panel by Jehan Fouquet in the Museum of Antwerp

crating his devotion to her, he learned how to control his passion which never betrayed itself before others.

§   §

The King and the court seemed to be at peace in beautiful Touraine. There was no longer the sound of arms, but, as Georges Chastelain said, around Agnes there was the "sound of women." It was heard in their childish prattling, their light laughter, the rustling of their brocades, in their boxes of Oriental perfumes, in the yelping of their little dogs. Charles loved this graceful femininity, this atmosphere of elegance and refinement. Antoinette had come again to visit her cousin, not invited this time, but of her own accord, in pursuance of the design which she had secretly formed.

But in the midst of these delights, war again summoned the King forth. The English had just broken the truce. They were marching upon Fougères, threatening to take back the lands which had been snatched from them with so much difficulty. Charles called his council and the decision was passed to conquer Normandy. In a charming scene, drawn from life by a contemporary, Jouvencel, we see the favourite, always eager to urge her lover on to glorious deeds, encouraging him on his departure:

"After dinner when the King arose from the table, he withdrew to his chamber and the Queen with several ladies and damsels in her company came and indulged in much good cheer and many jests, as was the custom.

"Among others, one very fair lady spoke, saying to the king: 'Sire, I have heard very good news reported, God be thanked, take us along to the war, and you and all your army will be all the more valiant. Our presence will be worth more to you than you can think . . .'

"And the king replied: 'If all has not yet been gained, it would surely be well to take you along, for I know very well that everything would be vanquished by you and the other fair ladies now present; but Jouvencel would have all the advantage; we should never come off with the honours there.'

"And the lady replied: 'Sire, do not be concerned about this, do you think that you can be King without great trouble and responsibility? No, surely, there never was one so. Great kings have great work and great cares. You will find enough occasion to cultivate the virtues of fair ladies when you wish.'"

Immediately after this the brothers Bureau organized the artillery and prepared their plans with Brézé.

Jacques Coeur, the steward and treasurer, provided two hundred thousand gold crowns [8] for the expedition.

"Sire, all that I have is yours," he said.

On the sixth of August, 1449, Charles, dressed in his armour of war, left Chinon, sending back a regretful glance at the beautiful château of his repose and at her whose lovely face, framed in a high window, smiled adieu. Agnes, again with child, remained behind in Touraine.

The conquest of Normandy succeeded rapidly. Charles made his triumphal entry into Rouen on November 10th. According to his custom, he did not treat the inhabitants harshly, in spite of their long dissent. Brézé received the keys of the city, of which he was made Commander and soon after Seneschal.

The houses were adorned with banners with the royal crest, the bells joyfully rang out in honour of the city's delivery from the yoke of the foreigner. The procession advanced to the sound of the fifes of the minstrels, walking before the long, straight lines of lances. The Scotch guard accompanied the King who appeared beneath a dais carried by citizens of Rouen. He was mounted on a palfrey and clothed in blue velvet sprinkled with golden fleur de lys and lined

[8] The old French *ecu,* or crown, was worth from $1.50 to $2.20.

with crimson satin, with a tassel of gold and silk, and in front a golden clasp adorned with a fine diamond. He was surrounded by pages on horseback, arrayed in long red robes and bearing javelins. All who followed, commanders and marshals, princes and squires, were armed "in white," that is, in armour of polished steel gleaming in the light.

> Rejoice thou, free kingdom of France,
> God now is fighting for thee.

So sang Charles of Orléans in hatred of those who had so long held him captive.

Harfleur surrendered next.

Charles established his headquarters there and as a place of rest chose Jumièges. It was there that Agnes came to rejoin him, in spite of her advanced pregnancy. Was it, as has been stated, because she desired to warn him of a plot spun by the ever rebellious Dauphin which involved the King's life?

Or rather, since she had a residence at Vernon-sur-Seine, had she come there to be nearer her lord? In any event she rejoined him at this moment and spent the month of January, 1450, with him, installing herself at the manor of Mesnil, a country-villa of the abbots of Jumièges.

This celebrated abbey is reached from Rouen by the river Seine. Its long, winding ribbon loses itself in the rich verdure of the forest of Canteleu. Here it can be traversed beneath lofty trees a thousand years old where in times past the invaders from the north concealed themselves. Here one breathes the fresh scent of the oaks and the birches, mingling with the odours from the Seine near by; then one passes Duclair and Yainville and, by a route which slopes down in an abrupt descent, reaches the valley where the wonderful abbey of days long past, the days of Charles VII and his loves, spreads its beauties before the eyes.

To-day there remain only the open apses or the walls carved with sculpture, now eaten away by time, that serve as a support for ivy and other creeping plants. An arcade rising beneath the open sky seems like a window to heaven through which one expects angels to appear. A ruin of the cloister still remains with its columns, a flowering of stones which the forest is submerging little by little.

Here Charles rested to taste the joy of his last victories. Here his well-beloved Agnes, who had braved the perils of the roads to join him, passed the last days of her life.

Was she disturbed by the dark dealings of her

cousin? Did she divine the danger that was threatening her? Did she wish to assure herself of a fidelity which meant more to her than life? A secret presentiment warned her of her approaching end.

She was delivered of a daughter on February 9th, 1450, in the little manor at Mesnil and soon after suffered an attack of dysentery which brought her to the point of death.

Thereupon she piously made her will, naming as her executors Jacques Coeur, Maitre Robert Poictevin and Étienne Chevalier, ordering that they should act only according to the sovereign will of the King. She gave 60,000 crowns to the poor and made innumerable gifts to the abbey for masses to be said for the repose of her soul.

Then she began to read the prayers for the dying, copied in her own hand from the verses of St. Bernard, after which she piously received the last sacraments.

Then, as if the vanity of her past happiness suddenly was made clear to her, she, the fair, rose-coloured lady who had known all the joys of this earth—love, riches, the homage of many hearts, the grace and beauty of the body, the sweetness of friendship; she, the beloved of a king, adored by the poor, she, Agnes Sorel, Lady of Beauty, turning to the Seneschal of Poitou and to

Guillaume Gouffier, said very softly: "It is a little thing and soiled and smelling of our frailty."

Like her friend, the Dauphiness of Scotland, she might have added: "Fi de la vie!"

These were her last words and her last thoughts as she left this earth, without regret. With a loud cry, her soul parted from her body on the ninth day of February, 1450, towards six o'clock in the evening. She was forty years old.

·   ·   ·   ·   ·   ·   ·   ·

Antoine de Baïf wrote this tribute to her:

O Death, this fair beauty
By her sweetness should have softened thy cruelty.
But in seizing her ravenously, in the flower of her life,
Thy injury has not been so great as thy presumption.
For if she had fulfilled the whole round of the days
That were rightly hers in the course of nature,
Her fair features, her fair skin and her fair flesh
Would have undergone the slow injury of old age.
And her surname, the Fair, along with her beauty,
Would have been taken from her forever by men.

·   ·   ·   ·   ·   ·   ·

The King was overwhelmed with grief.

When he had kissed her lips, the lips which had spoken so many words of consolation, good counsel, tenderness and graceful compliment to him, the lips now cold and blue forever, he said: "It is my wish that she be buried like a duchess." And he bestowed upon her the title at this moment. When he left her side, the monks began the funeral services. According to his wish, her heart was taken from her body. Her heart was left at Jumièges, her body borne along the rough roads to Chinon, there to enter upon its last slumbers.

> Here lies Agnes Seurelle, Lady of Beauty—
> Here lies the noble lady, Agnes Seurelle . . .

The monks of the collegiate church of Loches came to the obsequies along with the lords from the court at Touraine. Queen Marie, it is said, long wept over her cherished friend who had never grieved her in a situation so difficult for both.

> Here lies:
> The noble lady Agnes Seurelle.
> In life Lady of Beauté, of Roquesciere,
> Of Issoudoun, and of Vernon-sur-Seine—
> Pitiful towards all people
> She who gave generously of her wealth to the church
> And to the poor
> .   .   .   .
> Pray to God for her. . . .

§   §

Let us leave in her eternal repose the gentle woman who was so greatly beloved and who deserved to be

THE TOMB OF AGNES SOREL AT LOCHES

loved, Agnes, named after the lamb, who served
France not by her ideas, but by her presence alone.
So many favourites have ruined kings by their ambitious love that she who saved a king by her love,
clothed in kindness, should at last be recognised. She
was beloved of men, she was beloved of God, for she
was allowed to disappear from this earthly scene before her beauty yielded to the attacks of time. So it
has remained imperishable in the memory she left
behind. She disappeared before her love yielded to
the inevitable assaults of jealousy and time. She was
mourned with tears by her lover, the King, whom
she might perhaps later have wearied with her own
tears and weighed down with complaints or remorse.

So she was successful in her death as in her life without her own striving, and has left to the world a vision
of her pure countenance and her bosom, soft and fair
as a flower.

But her death, coming on so swiftly, left the field
free for all sorts of legends. It was at once reported
that she had been poisoned. The rebel Dauphin was
the first to be accused. Jacques Clerc has written as
follows of this matter: "And they said too that the
said dauphin had caused the death of a lady named

Agnes, who was the fairest woman in the kingdom and greatly in love with the King, his father."

Jacques Coeur also was accused.

What is to be thought of these assertions? Charles VII ordered an investigation. The very fact that he thought these accusations worth crediting proves that they were plausible. But they were false, without a doubt. If it is certain that the Dauphin detested the favourite, slandered her, insulted her and that, to reach the throne more quickly, he was capable of many things, even an assassination, that is saying a great deal. But the actual fact remains hidden in mystery.

As to Jacques Coeur, the matter cannot even be seriously considered. He was a friend of the Lady of Beauty, he attained his lofty position at court and in the council of the King through her influence; their understanding and their affection remained invulnerable until the end. What possible interest could he have had in killing her? Agnes named him as one of the executors of her testament—was this not in itself proof that she was sure of his devotion? The very suspicion is absurd.

It is probable that she died a natural death. Pregnant and forced to travel the long roads from Touraine to Normandy in uncomfortable wagons and litters in order to rejoin the King, she must have been exhausted by her journey and perhaps she caught an infection during her difficult confinement. Her little daughter died soon after birth.

We must set aside, we feel convinced, the idea of an assassination and believe rather that the unfailing good fortune which attended Agnes from the cradle to the tomb granted her this premature death which has bestowed on her eternal youth in the memory of men.

§　　§

Charles VII with heavy heart had to continue the Norman campaign. The English descended upon Cherbourg. The French halted their advance, seizing Formigny, Avranches, Bayeux, Valognes. Thereupon the King returned to Montils and remained there during the following months, preparing for the campaign of Juyenne. In less than two months, his commanders, Dunois, Xaintrailles, Armagnac and Foix, conquered the last province to be held by the enemy.

The Hundred Years' War was ended.

Then, as if with the unpleasant memories of this long struggle which had filled all his life, he wished also to live over the pleasant ones which had aided him in surmounting all obstacles, Charles VII came to the château of Taillebourg with his daughters by his beloved mistress. Here, by their side, he remained several months.

He had ten more years to live. Ten years without Agnes, whose bright smile and soft voice had lent magic to all his days! With what despairing tenderness he must have looked at Charlotte, Marie, Jeanne, three rosebuds sprung from a crimson rose-tree, three princesses of the blood of France, three children of a great love . . . In watching their movements, in hearing their words that seemed like echoes of the fair, enchanting beloved, what poignant distress must have filled his soul. . . .

Kings are men and men are all alike.

After all, it was scarcely strange that his factitious energy, which had only been sustained by the will of another, should disintegrate. His energy had been too long strained, too many assaults on it had exhausted it. His "good mother" Yolande, who had made him "the Victorious" and "the Well-Served" was no longer near him, nor she who had been placed beside him to restrain his perverse instincts and rouse him from his feeble indifference.

The King, Charles VII, at his château of Taillebourg, beside his daughters Charlotte, Marie, and

Jeanne, must have felt that he was dying of dreary loneliness. He was once more drifting, as at the time when, as Count de Ponthieu, he saw himself disinherited, abandoned, wretched, in his chaotic realm.

The result of this natural depression probably explains the events that now followed. Those who are unwilling to concede the happy influence of the favourite on the King can none the less not deny that the period of restored character and discipline in the life of the destitute prince corresponds exactly with the reign of Agnes over his heart. As soon as she disappeared, he fell back into his errors and his excesses.

Is it not natural to see in these excesses the effect of a melancholy disposition seeking to flee from itself, to lose itself in facile and intemperate pleasures? Is it not natural to accept the fact that the period of action, of wisdom, of victory of this King of France was due to the love he bore his mistress, a love founded on delight, but also on friendship, trust, and happy relaxation? The smile of the young beauty, her sweet temper, which all felt and by which all men, whether king or merchant, were charmed, had exerted a magic spell.

When Charles returned to Chinon, the château lacked her radiant presence. He wandered through the great halls, a prey to mortal weariness. He was soon surrounded and watched by a swarm of young girls, the attendants of Agnes and of Margaret of Scotland. There was Préjente de Melun, there were Jeanne Filleul, Marguerite de Salignac, Jeanne and Annette de Guise. Charles diverted himself with them, warmed himself by their youth and their affection. But he needed more to fill the immense emptiness left by the vanished tenderness of the woman he loved.

And now the cousin of the departed favourite appears at court, who resembles her without being like her—Antoinette de Maignelais.

She has awaited her hour and now it is at hand. She triumphs at the last. The rivalry between the two women here reaches its natural epilogue. But while Agnes had made her love the means of the King's moral regeneration, a motive for enthusiasm and exaltation, Antoinette, possessing herself of him in the decline of his life, made hers a means of dissoluteness.

Charles did not resist her advances, he abandoned himself to their evil influence; he was not strong enough to resist the assaults of a pretty woman determined to conquer him. He married her off to a complaisant gentleman, one of the companions of his early debaucheries, André de Villequier, called "the King's darling." He gave him as much money as he wished,

made him Count de St. Sauveur, Governor of La
Rochelle, with the revenues of Oleron, Marenne, etc.
The marriage was celebrated at Montbazon at the end
of October, 1450, and Charles remained there with
Antoinette for two months. It was she who was to be
the future queen of the court. She presided over jousts
and festivities. The King presented her with the city
and Seigneurie of Issoudoun which had been his gift
to Agnes. He offered her the château of la Guerche in
Touraine. Antoinette accepted his favours and occupied his time. He remained invisible for days; she
became all powerful through her vices and her complaisance.

"Wherever the King went," says Thomas Basin, "he
had to be followed by a flock of women, in all the
luxury and pomp of queens."

There were of course many fast women, too, such
as "Marion, the workwoman, Alison, the laundress."

The ambassador from Milan wrote at this time:
"The king of France is wholly given over to women."
To women and to jesters, we may add, who appeared,
or rather began to reappear at this time. They reappeared with their bells, Dago and Robinet and Michon.

Like the Pompadour, Madame de Villequier constituted herself procuress for the aging king who wanted

only to escape melancholy and boredom. One anec-
dote, recounted by the chronicler Jacques Clerc in
1455, is well-known:

The daughter of Antoine de Rebreuves of Arras,
named Blanche, came to the court accompanied by
Madame de Genlis. Blanche was young and most
beautiful. Antoinette de Maignelais having noted her
begged Madame de Genlis to entrust the young girl
to her. But she refused, saying that she could make no
arrangements about the young girl without her father's
permission. This gentleman had fewer scruples and,
having been informed of the favourite's offer and all
that she promised, he hastened to acquiesce, receiving
a fine recompense for his complaisance. Blanche's
brother, aged twenty-seven, took his sister back to
court again and entrusted her to Antoinette. The
young girl wept and struggled against her fate, saying
that she preferred to remain poor all her life rather
than undergo this shame, but all was in vain. She had
to submit to the King's advances and made the fortune
of her family, remaining in Charles' seraglio, well
provided for by his mistress.

The love of Agnes had made Charles a knight.
That of Antoinette made him a debauchee.

He became restless and his former phobias returned.

Disturbed and nervous, he could no longer remain long in one place. Now he was at Montils, now at Montbazon, at la Guerche, at Bois-sur-Aisne, at Chissay with his paymaster Pierre Berard, or at Montrichard with the Countess of Tancarville. He was prodigal and extravagant in satisfying his desires. Every year he gave to Antoinette a diamond worth seven hundred crowns. His accounts reveal his weaknesses. The sisters-in-law and the sister of the new favourite were loaded with favours. Thoine de Villequier received a gold chain worth two hundred and seventeen crowns and, in the following year, two hundred crowns. In 1454 she received a chain of gold enamelled in the colours of the King and marked in Saracen letters. The King himself was mad about clothes. His accounts show that in one year he paid for twenty-seven robes of silk and velvet and fifty of wool, without counting head-coverings and boots.

On July first, 1454, André de Villequier, whose complaisance had paid so well, died. To console the widow, Charles shut himself up with her in the manor of la Guerche, bestowing on her the right to its succession and two thousand *livres* to keep up the state of a queen. From that time on no one was able to put a limit to his dissolute life. It would have needed the firm will of Yolande, the love of Agnes to direct him. He was entirely delivered over to his favourites, he became the prey of those who exploited him. His son was far away and caused him only trouble, his other children were married or too young.

After the death of the Lady of Beauty, the King and Queen lived apart. Marie of Anjou apparently ceased to care what became of her husband, since she knew very well that she had no power to restrain him. She lived in state at Chinon with her two young children and a young daughter whom she had adopted, Louise de Laval. She had her chaplains, her women, her physician; she had a passion for animals. Her son Louis inherited the same taste from her. Dogs, hinds, goats, hares, parrots disported themselves in the great hall at pleasure. Marie adored jewels, precious stones, richly illuminated books.

After Villequier's death, Charles called her back to be near him. Was this because of a belated regard for respectability, or because of his feeling of loneliness? In September she started forth with all her household and went to Mehun, where the King was sojourning with the chief favourite. Did he wish to see his children, perhaps, or was he silently demanding aid against those who controlled him and against whom he was unable to defend himself? The Queen knew nothing about this or did not wish to know anything about it, for she treated the favourite affably. If she did not go so far as to give her friendship, as she had done with Agnes, at least she acted generously towards her husband's mistress. In her accounts there is found this description of a gift she made her for the New Year:

"For the ornaments of a glass fountain very richly wrought, entirely surrounded with delicate workmanship in leaves, in the form of a crown, and surrounding this fountain four gargoyles of gold very gracefully made, from which pours the water of this fountain, and above, the cover adorned with the same ornamentation and workmanship. And above the base of the fountain, there is the same ornamentation as above; above the base of the fountain there are four golden lions very gracefully wrought which support the said fountain."

"Given the said day as a New Year's gift to Mademoiselle de Villequier." The gift was truly royal, if not conjugal.

So the court was complete now at Mehun: the King, the Queen, the princes, the favourite, and the seraglio. There they lived together at the end of this long reign, so crowded with tragedy and so profoundly immoral.

Contemporary writers testify to the dissolute life of this time with sorrow: "The said Charles the Seventh, after he had driven forth the enemy and brought peace to his kingdom, was not exempt from many misfortunes, for in his old age he lived luxuriously and too carnally with women of bad reputation and evil life, with whom his house was thronged. And his barons and servitors, following his example, gave up their time to pleasure, dancing, mummery and foolish love."

What more perfect tribute could there be to her who had maintained him for nearly seventeen years in the grandeur and dignity necessary to victory? There can be no doubt that without Agnes he would never have accomplished the surprising prodigies of his reign, rich in miracles. A contemporary tries to excuse him and gain indulgence for him on the ground that the unnatural effort which he had to make to conquer himself and his kingdom caused the sudden failure of will later. His organism was not made to resist these intimate, social battles.

"For the great work which the King had done in reconquering the greater part of his kingdom, he was resolved to have the most beautiful girls that could be found."

§   §

This relaxation of morals had its natural reverberations in affairs of state. Charles VII's character, supported in other days by forces outside himself, enlightened by minds better informed than his, could not of itself maintain the justice and equity which had marked his active, fruitful years. He was not wicked, but weak. Being weak, he became ungrateful. The moment came when he committed the second great fault of his reign. Just as he had abandoned Jeanne d'Arc, the saint who had made his victory possible, he now abandoned Jacques Coeur, his able steward and treasurer, who had supplied him with the funds necessary for the revival of the sorely wounded kingdom. Jacques was Agnes' friend, but Agnes was no longer present to sustain him. Jealous enemies who had long envied him his favour and his fortune now made use of the King's weakness to strike him down.

He had become embarrassing by his presence and his immense wealth. He no longer left the King, who was watched by opposing interests. It was said that his fortune in France was worth a million in gold. He

possessed in addition la Chastellenie, the land and
Seigneurie of St. Fargeau, Champignolle, Mazilles,
Villeneuve, les Genets, Melleroy, Fontenailles, Toucy,
Villebon, Boulaincourt, la Fresnay, Roannais, etc., etc.,
etc. More and more he was surrounded by hatred, because he was the creditor of all the great seigneurs, as
he was of the King. Precisely those who owed him
most were most rabid in desiring his ruin, since they
despaired of ever repaying him otherwise.

Undoubtedly a fortune so vast is not acquired without risks and secret wrongdoing. That is the story of
all financiers. But this fortune benefited the realm
and it was admired and looked upon with wonder so
long as it served the realm. When it was no longer
so greatly needed, it became suspect. Warnings were
given to the steward which he disregarded, believing
himself strong in his credit and in the services he had
rendered. The vultures continued to watch. He was
the banker of the whole court. Furthermore, he was
one of the new rich. He bought up the lands of the
nobles ruined by the war and unable to raise themselves above the ruins. His most implacable enemy,
however, one determined to bring about his destruc-
tion, was an Italian, Otto Castellani, who in the name
of his Genoese compatriots, commercial rivals of the

steward in the Orient, fomented his downfall to profit their own business.

Thereupon words of poisonous suggestion were whispered into the King's ears along with suspicions, looking to the past, on the subject of Agnes' fidelity, whose good understanding with the steward was well-known. Had the King then been deceived? He was also informed that Jacques was allied with the rebellious Dauphin and was supplying him with funds. All this touched Charles VII in his two most sensitive spots—his mistress and his son. Finally Jeanne de Vendôme started the report that Agnes had been poisoned by the steward. The reports were absurd and contradictory, but pretexts were wanted by the vultures, greedy to fall upon their prey. The possessions of Jacques Coeur were sequestered; soon after he himself was seized and imprisoned, first at Taillebourg, then at Lusignan.

Accusations against him multiplied: he was charged with supplying the infidels with war material, with debasing the currency, and with malversation in Languedoc. The chief charge, that of poisoning Agnes, was still maintained.

Before this greedy horde, Jacques Coeur first denied, then confessed everything that they wished. While in prison, he lost his wife whom he loved; nothing more remained to him in the world, after all his unlimited power. He said what they wished him to say, in the depths of a physical and moral depression brought on by such great injustice. He had said to the King, when giving him the money for his wars: "Sire, all that I have, is yours." And Charles VII, taking advantage of this imprudent speech, took all, even the honour, even the life of this faithful servant, to please others who envied him and owed him many benefits. Suddenly even his skill in finance, of which all had made such far reaching use in difficult times, was suspected. It had now been exploited; it was therefore no longer necessary to admit that it existed. He had been indispensable, now he was in the way. His services had passed beyond the limits of gratitude and were crushing those who had made use of them. That is to say, Jacques Coeur was now judged by his debtors, who in this way would not only be freed from the obligation of paying their debts, but would also share in the spoils of the vanquished.

Unquestionably the princes and nobles would not have been able to do anything against him if the King had not been struck with incurable weakness. They had been forced to await the death of Agnes Sorel before they could attack this quarry. They had waited also until Otto Castellani, in turn, should promise them new benefits which could no longer be gained from the steward. Without realising that this shrewd Genoese was sweeping his most formidable rival off the market, to the detriment of France, Jacques Coeur was pronounced "unfit to hold any royal or public offices, and condemned to make public amends to the person of our public prosecutor, bareheaded, without head-covering or girdle, on his knees, holding in his hands a lighted torch of six pounds of wax, etc., etc. . . ."

This was a humiliating condition for the lord of so many lands, the sumptuous host of the Hôtel de Bourges, the man who had scattered precious stones among his friends, the goldsmith who had adorned the ladies and the princes with marvellous jewels and had perfumed them with all the scents of the East.

On July 5th, 1454, in the presence of a large crowd, the former royal steward and treasurer, equal of lords of high degree, friend of the Lady of Beauty, he who had revived the financial security and the commerce of the stricken kingdom, in this enforced condition of shame and humiliation cried: *"Merci à Dieu, au roi et à Justice!"*

Then began the scramble for the booty, his enemies
serving themselves well, with Charles VII in the lead.
But the victim, though he was brought down to the
earth, was still a colossus. He knew that nothing is
wholly lost so long as life remains in the body. He
knew that the intention of all his enemies was to have
him disappear secretly. So, while he was shut up in
the château at Poitiers, he escaped in October, 1454,
sought refuge in a monastery at Montmorillon, wandered about the country as a beggar, hiding in the
forests, until he finally reached Beaucaire. He was of
course pursued and tracked. One day in a church he
was recognised and attacked. He defended himself
with the blows of a lead mallet and escaped again. An
attempt was made to poison him. Then he decided
to leave France forever. At Marseilles, where he had
flourishing counting-houses, he also had friends who
chartered a galley in which he sailed for Rome. He
found safety in the papal possessions. The King's
agents who pursued him had their trouble in vain.
Pope Nicholas, mindful of past services, became his
protector.

But Jacques Coeur was ill, exhausted, alone, separated from his children. He had only his indomitable
courage left. His friend, Pope Nicholas V, had at this

time formed the plan of another crusade against the infidels. He died without fulfilling his vow, but his successor took up the idea anew. He entrusted the management of this undertaking to Jacques Coeur. A fleet of sixteen galleys was equipped, with the former treasurer in command, with the title "Captain-general of the Church against the Infidels."

Hardly had the fleet reached the island of Chios when Jacques Coeur died on November 26th, 1456. He was buried in the Franciscan church. With his last words he commended his children to the King: "Begging him humbly, in consideration of the great possessions and honours he had attained in his time near the King's presence, that it would be his pleasure to provide for his children enough so that those who were laymen could gain an honest living, without falling into want."

An astonishing story this of a remarkable man who has not received his proper share of glory! Lamentable ingratitude of a King, to be repeated again and again by his successors, under similar circumstances! Jacques Coeur was a great Frenchman. If he increased his own fortune at the same time as that of his country, should his country take him to task for this? He was a modern man, with all the boldness, all the recklessness, all the willingness to run a risk, but also with all the greatness of the modern man. Louis XI who vindicated his reputation understood men. He made the families which had despoiled Jacques Coeur return the estates which they had seized and he restored to the steward's children the rights and goods which had been confiscated.

The two blots on the reign of Charles, his two acts of ingratitude, towards Jeanne d'Arc and Jacques Coeur, occurred before and after the coming of Agnes. So long as the gentle lady with the clear glance influenced him, the King was great and magnanimous. She raised him above himself. Feeble, "mutable," a victim of his own nature, he was saved by her true love. After her death, he was again only a beast let loose, given over to his worst instincts. Only death would end his downfall.

§   §

His last years dragged on pitifully. With his train of women he went from château to château, inaccessible to his people, consumed with sorrow and anger caused by the hatred of his son, the Dauphin, now fled to Genappe in the lands of the Duke of Burgundy. Without his father's consent, Louis had just married

Charlotte of Savoy, and he continued to spin his secret intrigues around the feeble King. From fear of being poisoned by the Dauphin, Charles refused to eat and almost died of hunger. Embassies to bring about a reconciliation passed incessantly from France to Flanders and from Flanders to France without restoring peace between the two irreconcilable foes.

"Bring peace to the fleur de lys," the little Dauphiness had said when she was dying. The fleur de lys was torn to pieces now. The King even thought of transferring the succession to the crown to his youngest son Charles.

Antoinette de Maignelais did not even manage to remain faithful to him. After 1459, though still chief favourite in name, she left the poor, sick prince, prematurely an invalid, to become the mistress of Francis, Count d'Etampes, later Duke of Brittany. By him she had two sons. Deceiving Charles as a lover, she betrayed him as a king too. It was she who kept up a secret correspondence with the Dauphin, supplying him with information which might aid him in his intrigues. Eager to strike a fatal blow at this father who delayed too long in surrendering his place, Louis informed him secretly of Antoinette's shameful conduct. Charles suffered such sorrow from this that it hastened his end.

A wound on his leg now became cancerous. An abscess formed in his mouth and in July he began to approach his end.

"What day is it?" he asked the priests who surrounded him.

"Sire," they replied, "it is the day of the blessed Madeleine."

"Ha-a . . . I praise God and thank him that it has pleased him to let the greatest sinner in the world die on the day of the great sinner."

Convinced that he had been poisoned by his son, he added: "I leave it to God to avenge my death."

He died on July 22nd, 1461, at Mehun-sur-Yèvre in Berry, deserted by all. Only Dunois followed his funeral.

§   §

Both are dead. Peace to their souls. They are no longer aught but unsubstantial shades floating in the empyrean, but their history, mingling for a brief space with that of France, deserves our interest and attention. It deserves, too, that we pause for a moment to throw a glance backward which will enable us to judge them fairly. For if in these pages their intimate story, the recital of their faults and their virtues has been emphasised, we may now consider the public result of their private association, quite independently of their secret, human joys and sorrows.

Agnes Sorel was a charming woman who fulfilled the mission for which she had been created, the mission of love placed at the service of the realm. An instrument in the hands of Yolande of Anjou, she herself possessed no rare political qualities to merit exaggerated praise. She was in no way a statesman. She merely made possible the activities of another, greater than herself, in her special field. She was soft, tender, good, and cheerful. In the happiness she bestowed on the King, he found his strength and support. It is on this account that she deserves our praise.

Charles VII is difficult to judge. A small character, he became, none the less, if we consider the results of his reign, a great king. We have seen his weaknesses, his incapacity. The weight of a bad ancestry rested upon him. He strove to rise above his wretched state, to stand up proudly in his tattered purple, to be firm and victorious. Great? His reign was more, it was a wonderful reign.

No nation had ever fallen so low as France under

the combined ills of the English rule and the rivalry of parties bent upon destroying one another. Charles on his father's death found everything in chaos. It was a reign of miracles; but only miracles that are possible really come about. It was Yolande, "the good mother," who made these miracles possible by welcoming Jeanne d'Arc, by becoming the patroness of Agnes Sorel. Through these two, by different ways, France was saved. Thereupon, aided by his supporters, Richmond, Brézé, Jacques Coeur, Bureau and others, Charles VII reconquered his kingdom; he did more, he organised it, a far longer and more difficult task.

The feudal lords were reduced in power, commerce was revived, the arts were restored to life. The King was devoted to letters and to history. He founded universities at Caen, Poitiers, Bordeaux; he kept an eye upon the editing of the Chronicles of St. Denis and had chapters of this work read to him; he was a patron of poets, he aided translators of ancient works, he encouraged the sciences. Cathedrals that had been halted in their upward flight by the long, destructive war, rose once more. Full of forbearance and kindness, he made an effort to lead the artisans back to their trade, the peasants to their tillage; he reorganised the public fairs and stabilised the depreciated currency. It was an immense work, an immense victory! . . .

To him was due the creation of a regular army. Henceforth the soldiers no longer were dependent on the great feudal lords, more or less hostile to the crown, but on the King himself. By a treaty with the Swiss and the Scotch he created an infantry. Under Charles VII France had the finest army in the world. Thanks to a prodigious effort between 1429 and 1461, thirty years repaired the ruins of a century. The "little King of Bourges" had become the great King of France. Thus his prestige became unequalled in Europe. He exercised authority in Lorraine, in Italy, in the East. The popes instigated him to give an example to other rulers in instigating a new era of the crusades. The doge of Venice said: "He is the king of kings, nothing can be done without him." Charles VII imposed himself as arbiter between Freiburg and the Duke of Savoy, between the Archduke Sigismund and the Swiss cantons. King Ladislaus addressed him in these words: "You are the pillar of Christianity and my suzerain lord is its shield. You are its house and my lord is its wall." The Emperor of Trebizond and the King of Persia, in making an agreement, declared that they were demanding nothing more than the aid of the King of France, whom they also called king of kings, and along with this, they said that the flag of the King of France and a commander to represent him would be worth more than a hundred thousand men. The caravels of Jacques Coeur bore the fleur de lys to the Far East, to the very gates of India.

It was a great reign, a reign of miracles, because the King was able to find strength in his private happiness, bestowed by the woman he loved, a woman who inspired him with the wise, strong suggestions whispered into her ear by servants of the state allied with her and devoted to the realm. The consequences of this love were overwhelming, for in affairs of state as in life, small causes often engender the greatest results.

Let us render homage to her whose soft smile scattered the dark shadows of war and anarchy.

We may note, in addition, that the Dauphin, her bitter enemy so long as he himself did not occupy the throne, changed his tactics as soon as he became king under the name Louis XI. He became the guardian of the memory of the Lady of Beauty and the protector of her daughters, his natural sisters, whose legitimacy he confirmed. In rehabilitating Jacques Coeur, the friend of Agnes, he put the stamp of royal approval

LOUIS XI, KING OF FRANCE
From the Contemporary Portrait at Château de Saint-Roch

upon her political alliance with the steward. In making Étienne Chevalier his ambassador and private secretary, he accepted her selection and continued her work through him.

When he visited the church at Loches, where Agnes is interred, the canons, thinking to flatter him and ungrateful to the memory of their benefactress, asked his permission to destroy her tomb, which was embarrassing to their church. With characteristic malice Louis replied: "That he would willingly agree to this, provided that they would renounce the legacy which she had made them." Naturally, the blundering canons did not insist upon their demand.

The tomb of Agnes remained there, to undergo the vicissitudes of time. On a slab of stone rests the statue of Agnes the Fair, sleeping, her hands folded, her head supported on a pillow. Two angels at her side are bringing her a ducal crown. At her feet watch two lambs, symbols of gentleness and goodness.

> O mors saeva nimisque jam juvenilibus annis
> Abstulit a terra membra serena suis.

Before turning away from her fragrant presence, let us place as flowers on her tomb, henceforward precious, the lines of Voltaire, the homage of France

to her who, with Love as her accomplice, served her
country so well.

> Never did love form so rare a lady.
> Imagine Flora in her youth,
> The form and air of a woodland nymph,
> And the enchanting grace of Venus,
> The alluring charm of love itself,
> Arachne's skill, the sweet song of the sirens,
> She had them all. In her chains, she would
> Have held fast heroes, sages and kings.

CHAPTER VI

The Children of Agnes
The Story of Charlotte of France

CHAPTER VI

The Children of Agnes
The Story of Charlotte of France

THE Lady of Beauty left three daughters by the King of France: Charlotte, Marie, Jeanne. A fourth, born in 1449, did not live and was the cause of her mother's death. What was the fate of the three young princesses, for as such they were known, after the passing of Agnes? While the King fell back into his early weaknesses, they had as their protector his wife, Queen Marie, who acted as a mother to them until her death. They had their father, too, for Charles, even in his darkest errors, remained faithful to the dear memory of his beloved. Finally, they had the support, quite unhoped for in view of the hatred with which he had pursued the Favourite, of their brother, the new King. Louis XI once firmly on the throne protected what he had fought so long: the blood of Agnes, because with it was mingled that of the King, his father. Just so he attacked the man who had supported him: the Duke of Burgundy. Opportunistic and subtle, he followed his policy of self-interest.

Marie, the second daughter, born in 1436, married in November, 1458, Olivier de Coëtivy, son of the Admiral Prégent de Coëtivy, who had reared her with devotion. Charles signed the marriage contract and presented his daughter with the château of Taillebourg and twelve thousand crowns, while he bestowed on her husband the title of Seneschal of Guyenne. Marie of Valois has remained a model of all the wifely virtues. She had her mother's beauty, sweetness and fidelity. Her correspondence with her husband has been preserved, exquisite in its delicacy and its devoted love. Their life together, passed in the country, is cited as an example. If the Seneschal was absent from home, a courier was despatched every day to give him news of his wife and his many children.

Jeanne, the third daughter, at twenty-one, married Antoine du Bueil, Count of Sancerre, son of the gallant knight who died in the tournament at Tours. The marriage, too, took place at Tours. She herself died very young, before the disgrace of Jacques Coeur, who had transferred to the daughters of Agnes the affection and the gratitude which he had felt for their mother. It was he who had a tomb erected for the young woman at Loches, near that of the Lady of Beauty. On it may be read these words: "Oh, Death, still inexorable, thou hast robbed life of so fair a body in its earliest years."

From these lines we gather that Jeanne was beautiful, like her mother.

Charlotte, the eldest daughter, whose tragic and true love-story we must now relate, was the especial favourite of her brother, King Louis XI. He married her to Jacques de Brézé, son of Pierre, Grand Seneschal of Normandy. That Louis on this occasion even departed from his avarice, his weak point, this document proves:

"I, Louis, by the grace of God King of France, to all whom it concerns, greetings: Be it known that in the marriage which has but lately taken place between our very dear and beloved natural sister, Charlotte of France, and the son of our loyal and loved knight, Pierre de Brézé, Count of Maulevrier, and for certain other favours and causes and reasons which move us to take this action, we have remitted, given over, bestowed and left, and we hereby now bestow, give over and leave, by special favour by these presents, to the said Pierre de Brézé and to his heirs and successors and assignees, the sum of one hundred Paris *livres* of revenue which the said Pierre de Brézé was bound to pay every year, on the first day of May, in return for the lands and Seigneuries of Nogent-le-Roi, Encret, Breval and Monchauvet, and the same revenue we have abated and we hereby abate by these presents to consist of a hawk, safely brought back, which shall be delivered by each from this time forward forever, to us and to our successors, the Kings of France."

All of which signifies, in this delightfully archaic language, that the King remitted the duties on these lands for all time.

§   §

History is life itself, but its events are connected. They mingle and explain one another. A character cannot fully be understood if it is isolated from its contemporaries; the importance of facts cannot be grasped if they are detached from what precedes and from what follows. I have already presented the lofty figure of Anne of France, Lady of Beaujeu, who continued the vast work of her father, Louis XI. She was a granddaughter of Charles VII, a great-granddaughter of Yolande, whose political genius passed down to her descendants. I have reviewed the case of Diane de Poitiers,[1] *Grant' Sénéchalle* of Normandy, unjustly re-

---

[1] See "The Moon Mistress: Diane de Poitiers, Grant' Sénéchalle de Normandy," by Jehanne d'Orliac.

garded as a courtesan by those who do not know of her noble birth, who helped to bring about in France a renaissance of artistic splendour.

Diane de Poitiers, then, was married to Louis de Brézé, son of that Jacques who married, as we have just seen, Charlotte of France, daughter of Charles VII and Agnes Sorel. There would be a blank between these studies of French favourites if we did not point the relation between the story of the Lady of Beauty and that of the Lady of Anet, between Agnes and Diane, through Charlotte of France, daughter of the one, mother-in-law of the other. Between the two brilliant stars, Agnes and Diane, whose love brightened the destiny of two kings, two who were victorious in life because the god of light love smiled upon them, we set a tragic lover, pitiful victim of her own heart, who did not know, like Agnes, her mother, and like Diane, her daughter-in-law, how to be "victorious over the victor of all."

So the mournful story of Charlotte of France stands here as a lament between two songs of joy.

§   §

Charlotte, who received the château of Beauté as part of her dowry, had the good fortune, or the ill fortune, to resemble her mother. She had her irresistible charm and above all that curious attraction which calls forth love, a dangerous gift which may lead to the greatest power or to the greatest misfortunes, according to how it is employed. Agnes and Diane understood how to attain glory by this gift. Charlotte gained only shame.

In her youth she lived at court with her mother, hunting with the King and playing her part at festivals and tournaments. Of all the princesses, she was said to touch the hearts of people most deeply. After her mother's death in Normandy she remained with Queen Marie and her father, who loved her for her resemblance to Agnes, for she had her mother's chestnut hair, her fair skin and her lovely, languishing eyes. Her two younger sisters married before her, probably because Louis XI was keeping her as a stake for some alliance favourable to his policies. For Louis a marriage was not a matter of sentiment but of interest. He proved this in the case of his own daughters, Anne and Jeanne, one of whom he betrothed to the Sire of Beaujeu, the other to Louis of Orléans, without troubling about their preferences and their happiness. By good luck, Pierre de Beaujeu had his heart in the right place and made Anne happy. By bad luck, Louis was an ambitious fool who made a martyr of his wife before casting her off.

For Louis, then, his sister Charlotte was no more than a bait, a political weapon. Through her he attached to his side a man who would serve him better because he was allied to him by marriage. For, on his accession to the throne, Louis, who had fought steadily against his father, took rough revenge on those who, in serving the late King, had opposed him.

Among these was Pierre de Brézé, Grand Seneschal of Normandy, grand master of the hounds of France, a comrade of Dunois, Xaintrailles and Jeanne d'Arc in the war. The new King had him imprisoned at Loches, famous for its dark dungeons.

Endowed with rare intelligence, however, Louis, when he had once proved that he was master and knew how to assure his authority, began to reflect that servants like Brézé were rare; furthermore, being a skilful hunter like his master, he would be very useful in hunting the deer and the wild boar and in guarding his realm. He decided to release the Seneschal if he would swear fidelity. Pierre, who felt no ill will towards the new King, agreed, inasmuch as it had not been Charles VII whom he had served so much as the King of France. His sword belonged to the ruler, not to the person. So a reconciliation took place and to seal it Louis gave his sister Charlotte in marriage to Pierre's son who in this way became brother-in-law to the King, a title not to be scorned.

Together they went to offer a prayer at the tomb of Agnes which stood not far from the place where the prisoner had suffered from Louis' vengeance.

Obviously, a marriage concluded in this way did not begin too auspiciously. Charlotte served only as the stake. She was twenty-six years old and she felt no love for her husband. But no one could oppose the King and, after all, the position she was entering upon was to be envied. However, brought up as she had been beside her mother, the Fairest of the Fair, with the homage which every one rendered her as a daughter of the King and of the all-powerful favourite, in the atmosphere of love and elegance which Agnes created around her, the young girl submitted without pleasure.

The marriage took place at Chinon in the château overlooking the Vienne. The bells of St. Étienne, St. Maurice and St. Mesmes pealed with all their might to inform the people of the great joy of this wedding festival of the King's sister and the son of the proud Seneschal. There must surely have been all the great people of Touraine present, hurrying to flatter the ruler to gain his favour. Heralds bore at the head of the wedding procession the coats-of-arms of the two contracting parties: the three fleur de lys of the royal house to which Charlotte belonged and the white pennon with eight blue cressets were mingled in their escutcheon, so that we find it again in that of Diane de Poitiers, with a still richer addition.

Pierre de Brézé, tall and imposing, was mounted on his charger. Jacques, his son, about to become brother-in-law of the King, bore himself proudly and wore a magnificent costume. Charlotte looked so much like her mother on this occasion that those who had known Agnes were surprised and delighted. But there was a shadow of sorrow on her face—a fact which also was noted.

In the midst of this brilliant cortège, dressed according to his custom in dark clothes, with his head covered with a fur cap adorned with medals, rode the King, the great King Louis, prematurely aged, puny and mean looking, hunched down over his saddle. Brooding over his own thoughts which never left him and over his plans to strengthen the monarchy, he told his beads and murmured his eternal paternosters. No one ever knew whether this was a pose or conviction, but in this way he concealed his intentions from the malicious who watched his every glance.

That evening there was a great feast at which the King was present. The King was fond of serving lavish repasts, although he himself was very frugal. To add to the gaiety of those present, he told some of the coarse, funny stories which he had heard at the Burgundian court where life was jolly and cheerful. He could recall them at will when things had gone as he liked and he told them in his soft "siren voice," which no one could resist.

"Everywhere, on the long tables arranged beneath the lofty panelling," says M. Edmond Pilon, "sparkled goblets and dishes of glass, while a profusion of game and venison was served on pewter platters . . .

"There were pastries of Touraine in the form of little ships with sails and flags . . . a deer, at the end of his race, cunningly made of sweets, and some very fine dogs, copied from those in the King's pack, also made of sweets, snapping at the deer's legs."

At that time they built dishes for the great feasts as they built churches. A fine pasty was a work of architecture as well as a temptation to gluttony; a master-cook was an architect as well as a cook. These cooks of the fifteenth century were full of pride in their calling, too. One needs only recall the reply made by a scullion of Plessis to Louis XI himself.

"How much do you earn?" the King asked him.

"As much as the King," replied the scullion.

"How is that?"

"The King earns his living and I earn mine."

This shrewd reply, which was of the sort that delighted Louis, pleased him so much that he gave the man a present, for he was a judge of men.

He was a judge of festivals too, which explains why he, who spent so little on himself, treated his court and his guests so lavishly when it seemed necessary, especially when he hoped to derive some benefit for his policy in this way. After the repast came the music. Then the dowry was counted out in sound money and good lands: forty thousand gold crowns, a dozen cups of silver, the gift of the city, and six goblets and ewers of silver.

Thereupon the King kissed his sister upon the brow, her two sisters did likewise, and the newly married pair was left to begin life together. It might well prove a difficult project.

§   §

Their domains were numerous and they lived in many places. Like Diane de Poitiers later, Charlotte was mistress of Anet, of Nogent-le-Roi, Montchauvet, Mauny, Bec-Crespin, as well as of Beauté which was her part of her maternal inheritance. With Jacques and her father-in-law, the Seneschal, she must often have stayed at the château at Rouen, where the Maid had died; but she preferred to live at Anet, which was then not yet the wonderful building erected by Philibert Delorme, but a fine château nevertheless, beloved of kings.

Charlotte, who resembled Agnes in features, had her kind heart also. The poor blessed her in Normandy, as they had adored her mother in Touraine. Like her future daughter-in-law, Diane, she loved the chase of which her husband was a master, and they entertained princely visitors who were passing through the country, at great cost to themselves.

In 1463 Charlotte had a son, Louis, of whom the King, Louis XI, was godfather. Hardly up again after her confinement, she received in Normandy Charles Charolais, the wild Duke of Burgundy, who was later called Charles the Bold. He was magnificently entertained, but his presence in this part of the country would have little importance in this narrative if he had not brought with him in his train, made up of numerous knights and attendants, a certain Pierre the apothecary, half astrologer, half physician, who was destined to destroy by his envy and jealousy a happiness which he could not hope to attain because of his ugliness. How did it come about that Pierre the apothecary, in the suite of the Burgundian, remained behind with the Brézé family? This has always remained a mystery. The most probable reason is that, as soon as he caught sight of Charlotte, he loved her with a love made up of hatred which some feel for the one whom they may never hope to attain. Charlotte, on the contrary, detested him as soon as she saw him.

At this time Pierre de Brézé was killed in the battle of Montlhéry (1465) and his son succeeded him as Seneschal of Normandy.

§   §

A new life now began for Charlotte, sister of the King, a life of social obligations and impersonal duties, with brilliant, official functions. We have no details of her private relations with Jacques. She had married him without love, she had children by him and seemed to feel respect and affection for him. He was above all madly devoted to hunting and has left us a book on venery which is full of information about that noble art, of which he was one of the glories. He was passionately devoted to Anne of France and absolutely faithful to the King who valued him for his qualities of endurance and persistence and for his knowledge of dogs, so useful in the sport of hunting. He must have been a bit rough and he was of course often absent from home. His wife gave him respect and affection, but was this love? Some part of our nature may remain unsatisfied, even in the midst of the greatest magnificence and honours. The ambitious are satisfied by glory. Others care little for splendour and renown and remain unsatisfied, even in a palace, if their heart is lonely. If by good fortune heart and pride are both satisfied by the same person, the result is that rare masterpiece, a successful life. This good fortune came to Agnes Sorel, the fair lady who found in Charles VII a lover and a King and who therefore deserves less credit for her fidelity since it was sustained by great material advantages. The same good fortune befell Diane de Poitiers, who was overwhelmed by Henry II with tenderness, riches, and love.

But Charlotte of France? Probably her husband, the mighty Seneschal, adored her. At any rate, she deserved this. She was beautiful. She had brought him, with the gift of her own person, the favour of her brother, the King. Was he tender, attentive? We have said that he was a great warrior, a mighty hunter. But does this make a lover? When a woman is a daughter of Charles VII, whose adolescence and later years proclaimed his abnormal inclinations towards pleasure, and of Agnes Sorel, whose contemporaries spoke of her sensual allurement, her compelling and irresistible charm, she probably bears in her own self the instincts for love which will one day demand satisfaction. But first he must appear whose irresistible passion will awaken the senses which have only been asleep.

At this time then, King Louis XI came to Normandy with his suite. He was a pilgrim always wandering through his kingdom. He was never to be found in the same place. Dressed in fustian like a peasant, he rode incessantly on a horse or a donkey, hunched forward over his saddle. He went from one end of France to the other to spy, to observe, to right wrongs, to watch, to look into the needs and the faults, the wealth or the poverty of his provinces, and to establish harmony, communications and equality between them. He created a post-system to improve the means of communication; fairs, to facilitate trade and exchange of goods. He was, as always, followed by people of the lesser nobility of whom he made up his train. He chose the members of the minor nobility in preference to the swaggering, ignorant princes, as they were for the most part, who were always exacting and always ready to rebel. He understood them well, since he himself had made use of them in the *Praguerie* revolt. He recognised in the middle-class citizens and merchants, his friends, the sound judgment and plain common sense which are needed to conduct affairs and business. From them he received the good suggestions of which he availed himself without appearing to do so and which he could reward without any danger of assisting a power which might hold his own in check.

So he arrived in Normandy with a small train, with the sole wish to hunt with the Seneschal, whose packs were celebrated. Louis loved animals passionately, dogs for their speed, cats for their feline grace, their wiles, their intelligence. His deep knowledge of men inclined him to prefer beasts. At Plessis his room was full of cats. At Chanteloup, at the edge of the forest of Amboise, he had established his "menagerie," consisting of all the rare animals which his emissaries were able to find for him in all Europe. The names of some of his dogs have been preserved.

. . . Baulde and Oyse,
Souillard and Lombard and Clairault-
Clerement, le Joussault, and Noyse,
Falloise, Fouillaulde and Myrault-
Vollant, Morrale and Marpault,
Souillard the nimble and Fricaulde-
Briffault, Moricault and Clairaulde.
All fine, stout, swift hunters—
Rameau, Rigault, and young Baulde,
Which three are sisters and brothers.

This doggerel is by Jacques de Brézé himself, who was
by way of being a poet in his leisure hours. He also
composed a song in praise of Anne of France, the beloved daughter of the King.

The King's pack was in charge of a squire named
Pierre de Lavergne, a tall, handsome young man of
serious aspect and fine, vigorous body. Charlotte must
have noticed him as soon as she saw him, for those
who are destined to love each other find each other at
first sight. But this strong, secret current of attraction
which unites two hearts is also often felt by a third
person, especially if this third person loves without
being loved in return. So it happened that the first
glance exchanged between the wife of the Seneschal
and the squire was caught by Pierre the apothecary,
who pursued without hope the lady of his dreams. If

he could not be loved by her he could at least prevent her from loving another.

The King, after a visit to Rouen, Nogent and Anet, and after hunting to his heart's content, felt that he must set forth again, indefatigable pilgrim that he was. He left with the Seneschal the young squire Pierre de Lavergne, along with the pack of which he took such good care.

Jacques de Brézé usually took de Lavergne along on his official rounds, but the young squire often remained at the château, too, and when he remained Pierre the apothecary took good care not to be far away. Before the lovers themselves had realised it the enemies of their love divined their sentiments and, because they disliked them, noted the preliminary signs. Madame de Brézé, of course, was always surrounded by her companions and her children, she read, she chatted and walked, without dissimulation. But casual meetings in long corridors of the castle, in the gardens, in the great halls cannot be avoided in the case of people living under the same roof. The squire and Madame la Sénéchalle, before they spoke, must often have smiled and exchanged silent greetings, or even have tried to see each other without saying anything, as is inevitable when a great mutual attraction exists between two beings destined for each other.

And when two seek each other, they find each other. In spite of the crafty surveillance of Pierre the apothecary, it is certain, as the old chronicles relate, that de Lavergne one day succeeded in speaking to his lady without witnesses. Was it perhaps in the interval of a chase? Was it in the garden or in the Thuillé wood, was it in the evening in the great hall as they watched, through the tall greenish window, the Norman twilight falling, heavy with the mists from the neighbouring Seine or the distant sea? The two lovers, it is certain, found each other alone for the first time, since there always is a first time, just as there must always be a last time in cases of this sort. It is love's fatality, the implacable course it must follow like the course of the river flowing from its source to its mouth.

Pierre de Lavergne was young and handsome, only a squire to be sure, but what does this matter to a heart that loves? We do not love a title, a crown, or a bag of gold; we love some one because of his hair in which our fingers can play as a musician plays on his strings. We love some one because of a brow, smooth as Italian ivory, because of hands as soft as flowers, because of a mouth sweet and fragrant as the pulp of a ripe fruit. We love because we love.

And Charlotte, have we not said, resembled her mother, known as the Fairest of the Fair—her whose soft bosom is offered as a temptation to the beholder in Jehan Fouquet's diptych and in the painting of the unknown painter—the bosom which ladies of that age did not hesitate to show to the eyes of all for their damnation? Charlotte did not love her husband, who had been received by her and accepted from the hand of her brother, the King, as a tool to achieve his secret political ends. At last the hour struck when she was to give herself of her own will, the only gift which lets us die without regret, if we have known it, because it has repaid us for the pain of living.

Then all the words that we have strangled burst from our lips with all the kisses we have saved, as an imprisoned swarm flies toward the light. Then we know why we are young, with warm, red blood coursing swiftly through the veins which, as we did not realise before, form around our body a dense network of blue paths, full of swift, tingling life. Then we know that our skin is sensitive, our eyes are bright, our teeth sharp. Then we know why we are alive, while before we only managed to exist. Charlotte now learned what had constituted her mother's glory and her good fortune and her legend. Like Agnes she loved, like her she was loved. . . .

But when the lovers at last were able to declare their mutual love, to reveal their naked hearts, promising each other to meet again with the help of their servants, they were being watched in the dark. Their secret, so long suspected, was known to the one who suffered most from this knowledge, Pierre the apothecary, left behind as a spy perhaps by Charles of Burgundy, now become Charles the Bold, implacable foe of France.

As for the young squire in love, who troubled little about statecraft, his only care was to meet his mistress again, to be near her, to see her. It was the hunts, especially, which gave him his opportunity, those splendid hunts like the one which has remained recorded in the memoirs of the period as the most perfect, on May 31st, 1477. The Seneschal was arrayed in leather and fine cloth. His wife was adorably beautiful on a mare caparisoned in velvet; Pierre de Lavergne handsome in his greenish-brown jerkin. They were attended by many invited guests who had joined their train at the sound of the horn, at the noise of the pack, in the early morning of this day before Trinity Sunday.

Oh! the intoxicating rides over the earth still damp

with dew, with the odour of the woods in one's nostrils and in one's ears the impatient roaring of the beasts, excited by the baying of the dogs! The intense joy of living, of acting, of breathing, especially when by our side is the being we love, who shares our pleasure and who alone, of all the futile crowd around, exists for us.

It is certain that Pierre de Lavergne and Charlotte took advantage of the hazards of the chase to meet secretly, to ride beside each other, to seize each other's burning hands, perhaps to bend forward and touch each other's fresh lips. In the ardour of their new love they forgot prudence and did not perceive that near them always suddenly sprang up the man who was hated and hateful, the apothecary with his dark designs, who weighed upon their joy like a heavy shadow.

Now on this same evening of the day of the hunt, the Seneschal and his guests, after the quarry had been gathered by torchlight, arrived at the château of Rouvres sur Vesgne, where the feast began. It was a fine banquet, in truth, to which every one did justice after the long day in the open air and the exciting chase.

Then came the hour for retiring, for every one felt

weighed down by the day's fatigue. The Seneschal, completely exhausted, threw himself upon his bed with his boots on.

As for Charlotte: "She heard him, the letters of pardon inform us, and she sent him word that she could not yet go to sleep with him until she had bathed and washed her hair."

And he, almost dead with fatigue, merely replied: "Very well."

So Charlotte left her husband resting, assured herself that he was sleeping heavily and went up to her own chamber.

"This was situated above the one in which the Seneschal was sleeping." Had she given her lover a rendezvous there? or rather, had he, in watching every step of his mistress and seeing that she was alone, wished to take advantage of this opportunity to see her again? She uttered a soft cry—half-unclothed, she faced Pierre de Lavergne standing before her and trembling with desire. How could she resist this appeal of the flesh, tingling with life after the day's exciting run, after the wines of the hunters' feast? How could they fail to take advantage of the slumber weighing down her husband, worn out from sheer exhaustion? They flung themselves upon each other, hungry for love, intoxicated with their youth, reckless and mad, satisfying themselves for all eternity.

So Agnes and Charles had done in their life passed at the châteaux of Chinon, Beauté, or Bois-Trousseau. So Diane de Poitiers and Henry II will do again in the years to come. Happy lovers they were who could at least show their love, to be glorified, not censured. These three were of a line of royal mistresses, a line whose hearts were insatiable, whose senses were prodigal—a wonderful trio of women beloved of love.

Midnight sounded from the belfry of the tower of Rouvres. Both Charlotte and Lavergne were so lost in their delight that they did not hear the shuffling sound of a step creeping near the door. This step went away quickly, descended the winding stairway, stopped before the door of the Seneschal and entered softly. Jacques de Brézé started up suddenly out of his heavy slumber. Then, in the silence of the night, Pierre the apothecary murmured a few words in his master's ear.

The Seneschal gave forth a roar like a wild beast and sprang up.

" 'Messire,' the traitor repeated very softly, 'she is with the squire, they are sleeping together, in her bed, they are committing adultery.' "

Jacques leaned against the wall to support himself.

He was still fully dressed and armed. He seized his broadsword, he seized his dagger, and, lighted by Pierre the apothecary, he went up to his wife's chamber, broke in the door with a thrust of his shoulder and stood before the terrified lovers. Charlotte cowered back against the wall. Lavergne, to defend her, threw himself upon the Seneschal who, before he had said a word, struck him so fiercely with his sword that the young man fell, rolling in his blood, with a heavy groan.

Then Charlotte arose to implore pity. " 'By St. John,' she cried, 'by St. John!' " . . .

But Jacques, drunk with rage, did not heed her appeal.

" 'Bastard! Oh, bastard,' he cried out. 'Bastard, Bastard!' " . . . Drunk and mad, he no longer remembered that she was of the blood of France but only that she was the daughter of Agnes, the favourite, the lady of love, the mistress of King Charles VII.

Then, writes Jean de Troyes:

"He seized her by the arm and dragged her to the ground and in drawing her down, he struck her with his sword between the shoulders, and then she went down to the ground and fell upon her knees."

The Seneschal, not moved by her beauty, or rather

exasperated all the more by this beauty because it was the cause of his dishonour, seized his hunting dirk and fixed it in her throat. And while she was still in the throes of death, he took up his sword again and ripped open her bosom.

Then he rushed out like one that is damned . . .

§   §

It is well-known how greatly King Louis loved his sister. When he heard of this horrible murder, he howled with despair and wrath. He, always so self-controlled, wept as he kept repeating: "Oh! the dog. Oh! the dog. . . ."

He decided that the Seneschal should have his head cut off. It was only with the greatest difficulty that he was induced to have this lord of the highest nobility, who was also his brother-in-law, tried by a court of justice. He resisted a long time, but at last, when he had become a little calmer, he consented.

But Louis was an expert in the art of torture. He knew that nothing so wears out a man, so racks him and reduces him to nothing, as a guilty conscience. Courage resists all assaults, courage can face death smiling; but courage wears out in long hours of solitude, when the same thoughts gnaw at the memory and fall incessantly upon the heart like drops of water falling upon a rock which they finally hollow out. Confined in the Conciergerie at Paris, Jacques de Brézé, who was now no longer Seneschal and whose property had all been confiscated, waited to be tried behind bars, waited six months at the pleasure of the King whom he had mortally offended. The summer passed, the autumn passed, November came with its chilling cold. Shivering with fever, Brézé stared at the walls of his cell and ruminated over his memories. Which were the most agonising? Those which recalled his happy hours or those which brought back his hours of sorrow? Remembering our hours of lost happiness tortures us more than recalling our hours of grief, if only because the former revive those moments of love forever vanished, love that filled the body with life and joy. . . .

Oh, the anguish as he thought of her body, of Charlotte, fair daughter of the fair Agnes! Her soft form, her exquisite bosom which the Seneschal had loved and which he had pierced in his outraged love! . . . Surely when he saw again in his mind her body in the arms of another, the prison and the cold must have seemed sweet to him, rather than that frightful moment when all was revealed to him. Rage got the better of him again, he roared like a wild beast as he had roared that night in the château of Rouvres, after the intoxicating chase.

At last came the day before St. Catherine's day, in the year 1477. Towards evening soldiers entered the Conciergerie and ordered the prisoner to follow them, in the name of the King. Jacques began to tremble, knowing Louis' implacable justice. He was willing to die, but not to suffer atrocious tortures, slow agony.

They made him get into a boat. "Are you going to drown me, sir?" he asked. But drowning was not part of Louis' plan. He was taken slowly along the Seine to Vernon, the castle given to the Lady of Beauty by King Charles. Vernon, the last station of her love, before she went to die at Mesnil, near Jumièges. Why did Louis send Brézé there? Was he to be tried here? No, not yet. Remorse, regret, relentless memory must first eat out the heart of the fierce Seneschal, slowly, surely, as mice gnaw the hard timber. Two years he remained imprisoned in this solitary castle, in the cold, in the north wind, in the heat of summer, in the growing sense of horror at his crime. His hair grew white, his flesh wasted away, he became mad, he called on death to release him. . . .

Then he was summoned forth a second time and in

this state, poor, pitiful, tottering, he was conducted to Nemours en Gatinais, where the King was staying at the time. Jacques dared to hope that he would be released at last. But no, Louis XI only had him brought before him, silent and tasting his venegeance to the full, so that he might contemplate his misery. When he had enjoyed this pitiable spectacle to the full, he had the prisoner conducted to Vincennes. There he remained again some time until he was taken back to Vernon, each time weaker, older, more and more ravaged. He was now only a mere shadow. . . .

It was at this time that a faithful old servant of his tried to help him escape. But Brézé was well guarded; the servant was seized and punished. Brézé only underwent more hardships as a result. His window was now closed up, the only light in his prison came from the fireplace. Jacques now began to lose his reason, he began to utter wild words. Then he was taken to Dreux, half dead, scarcely able to stand up, and next to the château of Lavardin at Vendôme.

Deciding that his victim had now endured enough during the long years of waiting in prison, the King ordered that the trial begin. It was brief since the unfortunate wretch confessed all and, now too weak to hate, could only burst into tears.

He was condemned to the loss of all his possessions
and to pay a fine of 100,000 gold crowns. His life was
spared, but he was left poor, naked, wasted, ruined.
So he was sent forth, utterly vanquished.

But life is always moving, fluctuating, changing. It
destroys what it has created and creates again without
ceasing new interests upon ancient disasters. When
Louis had sufficiently avenged the death of his sister
and his sorrow at her loss, extenuating it with the
years, he remembered that the Brézés were a proud
race of warriors and hunters, such as few could equal
in his kingdom. It would be well to husband their
blood. So the king restored to his nephew, Louis, the
son of Jacques, what he had taken from the father.
Louis in turn became Seneschal of Normandy, Seigneur of Anet, Mauny, Nogent, etc., etc. It was he
who in 1514 married Diane de Poitiers, daughter of
Jean de St. Vallier, who was faithful to him until his
death in 1531.

It was only after his death that she became the
favourite of Henry II and one of the line of royal
mistresses.

Jacques de Brézé later had the mortal remains of
Charlotte borne to the abbey of Coulombs, near
Nogent-le-Roi, where he himself was interred. So the

victim and the assassin repose side by side in death; while Pierre de Lavergne, the young squire, was flung into the ground like a dog, at Rouvres, where he had succumbed to love and to vengeance.

§   §

Such is the tragic story of Charlotte of France, daughter of Charles VII and Agnes Sorel. Her son, the Seneschal Louis de Brézé, and Diane, her daughter-in-law, had two daughters. Through these the blood of the royal favourite, the Lady of Beauty, is mingled with that of the greatest families of France, some of which exist to this day—those of Bouillon, Lorraine, Clermont-Tonnerre, Beauvau, Ligne, Mouy, Saxony, Spain and Savoy.

Through this last house her posterity has four times occupied the throne of France, in the persons of Louis XV and his three grandsons.

§   §

To love is not culpable in the eyes of men who are without pity and without mercy; but to love beneath one, with a great, disinterested love, sufficient unto itself, is counted shameful.

Between Agnes Sorel and Diane de Poitiers,

glorified because they were the mistresses of kings, glides the mournful shade of Charlotte of France, the mistress of a simple squire who paid for her weakness with her life.

INDEX

INDEX